LIFE WITH GOD

dwell

FOR THE WORLD

BARRY D. JONES

FOREWORD BY MICHAEL FROST

IVP Books

An imprint of InterVarsity Press
Downers Grove, Illinois

InterVarsity Press
P.O. Box 1400, Downers Grove, IL 60515-1426
World Wide Web: www.ivpress.com
Email: email@ivpress.com

InterVarsity Press® is the book-publishing division of InterVarsity Christian Fellowship/USA®, a movement of students and faculty active on campus at hundreds of universities, colleges and schools of nursing in the United States of America, and a member movement of the International Fellowship of Evangelical Students. For information about local and regional activities, visit intervarsity.org.

All Scripture quotations, unless otherwise indicated, are taken from THE HOLY BIBLE, NEW INTERNATIONAL VERSION®, NIV® Copyright © 1973, 1978, 1984, 2011 by Biblica, Inc.™ Used by permission. All rights reserved worldwide.

While all stories in this book are true, some names and identifying information in this book have been changed to protect the privacy of the individuals involved.

Cover design: Cindy Kiple
Interior design: Beth Hagenberg
Images: © ferlistockphoto/iStockphoto

ISBN 978-0-8308-3669-7 (print)
ISBN 978-0-8308-9654-7 (digital)

Printed in the United States of America ∞

Library of Congress Cataloging-in-Publication Data

Jones, Barry D., 1978-
  Dwell : life with God for the world / Barry D. Jones.
    pages cm
  Includes bibliographical references.
  ISBN 978-0-8308-3669-7 (pbk. : alk. paper)
  1. Christian life. 2. Jesus Christ--Example. I. Title.
  BV4501.3.J6425 2014
  248.4—dc23

                                                                      2014022812

P 24 23 22 21 20 19 18 17 16 15 14 13 12 11 10 9 8 7 6 5 4 3 2

Y 34 33 32 31 30 29 28 27 26 25 24 23 22 21 20 19 18

Contents

Foreword

I met Barry Jones at Dallas Theological Seminary in 2010. I had been invited to present some guest lectures to their students on the subject of Christian mission. Although my lectures had been arranged by the missiology department, I was aware that professors from other faculties had been encouraged to attend. So when Dr Jones introduced himself to me as a professor of pastoral ministries and spiritual formation I wasn't surprised, but the way he tells it I visibly recoiled. I guess that was because I'd become used to professors of spiritual formation being the last people to really get what I was talking about.

It might be a caricature, but from my experience the professors who teach pastoral ministries tend to be focused on preparing their students with the skills of self-care and the establishment of what they like to call "boundaries." They often seem oriented toward the inner work of self-reflection, contemplation and holiness. We missional types are more oriented to the outer work of service, justice seeking, peacemaking and evangelism. We're more in the "damn the torpedoes" category—ready to fix bayonets at dawn and storm any barricade. In other words, pastoral ministries professors make me nervous. And vice versa.

When Barry approached me that day after my lecture in Dallas, I might have been expecting some pushback from him about how us missional folks need to step away from unreflective and boorish ac-

tivism and learn to smell the roses. But instead what I got from Barry
was an invitation to dinner at a local Vietnamese restaurant. And a
pretty good one at that.

Barry and I shared more than a meal that day; we shared our hearts.
It had been my hope for some time that someone would write a theology of *missional spirituality*. Not a version of spirituality that values
withdrawal over engagement and pietism over practice, but a model
of spiritual formation that sees actional engagement in place and
among people as the very stuff from which godly formation can take
place. We need a radical spirituality of missional engagement, I
pleaded with him.

This, it turned out, was Barry's same desire. He had been tooling
around with the guided spiritual formation program at DTS, looking
for ways to integrate missional presence with the poor and the lost
into the processes of preparation for ministry. He saw justice seeking,
peacemaking and neighborliness as the contextual framework for the
reflection and inner work required of every follower of Christ.

That day, over a delicious bowl of pho, a friendship was struck and
I urged Barry to write something in this field. He took me seriously.

You'll note that the subtitle to this book is *Life with God for the
World*, and you'll find that phrase repeated throughout. That's not
simply a snappy title to grab a reader's attention. It is the very
framework of Barry's thesis. We were made for life *with* God (spiritual
formation) *for* the world (mission). Indeed, it is this very life that Jesus
came to secure for us, and it's for more of this life that we actively wait
in hope. To hear Barry tell it, living with God for the world is the key
to all human flourishing. It involves self-care and introspection, repentance and holiness, *and* place making, justice seeking, service and
evangelism. In this nexus lies the hope of real, abundant, rich, beautiful human existence. It's the place that Jesus modeled for us and
about which he spoke when he urged us to love God with all our
hearts and souls and minds, and to love our neighbors as ourselves. In

short it means to dwell—to be at home—with God and for the world.

A few years after that Vietnamese meal in Dallas I was honored to be on a panel assembled by IVP to judge book proposals. I was doubly honored to be part of awarding a contract to Barry Jones for the book you now hold in your hands.

I believe *Dwell* makes a profound and timely contribution to both missional and pastoral studies, and is written by someone who has invested many years into understanding how to dwell both *with* God and *for* the world.

Michael Frost
Morling College, Sydney, Australia

Introduction

The Incarnation and Christian Spirituality

*The Word became flesh and made his dwelling among us. We have
seen his glory, the glory of the one and only Son, who
came from the Father, full of grace and truth.*

JOHN 1:14

*Christianity is the story of how the rightful King has landed,
you might say in disguise, and is calling us all to take
part in His great campaign of sabotage.*

C. S. LEWIS

The most important moment in the birth of a child is the moment
when the little one lets out her first cry. It is the vital sign of life. In
fact, it used to be the common practice for doctors to help this
moment along by holding the newborn by her feet and slapping her
backside. While the practice offends some contemporary sensibilities,
it served a crucial function. At birth, a baby's lungs are filled with
fluid. The first cry helps expel the fluid and allows the baby to take
her first breath. The lungs expand. Oxygen rushes in. Respiration

begins. Her life in the world commences with the rhythm of breathing in and breathing out.

We rarely pay much attention to the rhythm of our breathing unless something interrupts it. But this rhythm pulses through every moment of our lives from the first cry of life until our dying breath. The average adult takes between twelve and eighteen breaths every minute, which means the rhythm of inhaling and exhaling occurs more than twenty thousand times every day. The rhythm of our breath is the rhythm of life.

There is a rhythm of life that pulses through the biblical vision of what it means to be human. A kind of breathing in and breathing out. An inhale and an exhale. The breathing in is our participation in the divine life. The breathing out, our participation in the divine mission. The breathing in is intimately connected to our experience of God's personal presence. It is life lived with God. The breathing out involves our participation in God's just reign. It is life lived for the sake of the world. The breathing in we often call "spirituality." And the breathing out we call "mission." The burden of this book is to show how these two—spirituality and mission—are intimately bound up with one another, like inhaling and exhaling. Further, I will be arguing that the embodiment of this breathing in and breathing out is of the essence of what it means to live a fully human life.

At the heart and center of the staggering story of grace told on the pages of the Bible is the claim that the God of the universe experienced that first rush of oxygen into his lungs when a peasant baby let out his first cry in a stable in Bethlehem two millennia ago. The single greatest difference between Christianity and every other theistic religion is succinctly captured in John 1:14: "The Word became flesh and made his dwelling among us." In the incarnation, Jesus embodied the breathing in and breathing out that constitutes the biblical vision of what it means to be human. In Jesus, the personal presence of God took on our humanity and "made his dwelling among us" in order to make a way for us to participate in the divine life. Throughout his life he modeled what it looks like to live in intimate connection with the Father and dependence on the Spirit. Through faith in his work on our behalf, we participate in the divine life and are filled with the indwelling Spirit, God's empowering presence. In his incarnate life, Jesus gave us the normative vision of spirituality, of life with God.

So too Jesus came, sent by the Father, to bring the just reign of God into the broken world subject to the reign of sin, death and the devil. The Christian story knows nothing of a detached deity who watches disapprovingly as the world he made spins madly on. As the Christian story goes, God does not stand at a distance merely watching the suffering of his creatures and the brokenness of his world. Instead he enters into that brokenness and takes on their suffering. He becomes a victim of human cruelty and injustice. In doing so he secures a hope beyond the brokenness of this world as we know it. In the incarnation of Jesus, God made his dwelling among us as the ultimate means of accomplishing his mission to rescue and renew his good but broken creation. Throughout his ministry Jesus called people to turn away from their other allegiances and to believe the good news that in him the reign of God had come near. After his resurrection Jesus commissioned his disciples, saying, "As the Father has sent me, I am sending you" (John 20:21). Jesus' incarnate life gives us the normative vision of what it looks like to live into the mission of God, of life for the world.

For the better part of the last decade I have served as a professor of Christian spirituality and a teaching pastor of a "missional church." In many respects it's been a great time to be engaged in both conversations. There has been in recent decades a renewed interest in Christian spiritual formation. The popularity of authors such as Eugene Peterson, Richard Foster and the late Dallas Willard has contributed to a resurgence in evangelical spirituality and the rise of a host of new voices who are adding depth and insight to the conversation. These authors have recaptured key aspects of the biblical vision and recovered rich resources from the Christian tradition for the contemporary life of faith.

At the same time the word *missional* has become an important part of the vernacular of many Christian leaders. Though the word seems to have been around for some time, it came to increasing prominence after the 1999 publication of *The Missional Church*, edited by Darrell Guder. In that book, a consortium of authors associated with the Gospel and Our Culture Network set out to bring the theology of such seminal missional thinkers as Lesslie Newbigin and David Bosch to bear on the North American context. Within a short period of time other strong voices emerged arguing for a complete reorientation of theology and, therefore, what it means to be the church centered around the *missio Dei*, the mission of God. Mission, they argued, was not just one of a number of things the church does. Mission is at the core of who God is and thus at the center of what it means to be the church.

In my roles as pastor and seminary professor, I have benefitted immensely from the many authors who have contributed to each of these conversations. I've read their books, attended their conferences and had the chance to develop personal friendships with several of them. But it has struck me as odd that, with only a few exceptions, these two conversations are being held without reference to one another. Those talking and writing about Christian spirituality are saying very little about mission. And those talking and writing about mission are making few references to Christian spirituality. This leaves both conversations impoverished.

A spirituality that is not inherently missional is a truncated vision of life with the triune God. At the same time, any vision of missional life or missional church that neglects the cultivation of dynamic dependence on and intimacy with the living God runs the risk of becoming mere activism. Spirituality and mission belong inseparably together, like breathing in and breathing out.

The central claim I make in this book is that the great need of the church in North America today is to recover a spirituality deeply informed by the logic of the incarnation. When I speak of the logic of the incarnation, I simply mean the implications of the incarnation of God in Jesus Christ for our thinking about Christian spirituality. The incarnation of the eternal Son, who took on flesh to accomplish our redemption, is a unique and unrepeatable event. But this event has far-reaching implications for how we understand what it means to be human and what God is up to in the world. The doctrine of the incarnation, affirmed and cherished by Christians in every time and place, needs to be translated into a corresponding way of life for those of us who claim to worship and follow the one who took on flesh. As Jacques Ellul has suggested, "A doctrine only has power (apart from that which God gives it) to the extent in which it is adopted, believed, and accepted by men [and women] who have a style of life which is in harmony with it."[1]

This book is about discovering that "style of life." Contrary to how some Christians choose to tell the story, Jesus did not come into the brokenness of this world just to secure for us salvation beyond it. He also offers a profound model for how he longs for people to live in the midst of this world's brokenness. He presents a model of how to dwell *with* God *in* and *for* the world. This is a book about becoming more like Jesus, about spirituality and mission belonging together like breathing in and breathing out. The logic of the incarnation points us to the indissoluble union between spirituality and mission.

A Christian spirituality that is deeply informed by the logic of the incarnation reminds us:

- *We dwell in this world.* It gives us a vision of the spiritual life that is profoundly this-worldly, having much to do with the day-to-day realities of life.

- *We dwell in this time and place.* It gives us a vision of the spiritual life that is inescapably concerned with when we live and where we live, our unique cultural moment and social location.

- *We dwell in these bodies.* It gives us a vision of the spiritual life that is adamantly embodied; it is concerned with the care of bodies (ours and others'), embodied relationships and bodily engagement in spiritual practices.

- *We dwell in this world that God will one day make new.* It gives us a vision of spirituality that is deeply attuned to God's purposes for the world, which involves an abiding concern with the brokenness not only in our own lives but also in the world around us.

As stated above, my central claim is that the great need of the church today is to recover a spirituality deeply informed by the logic of the incarnation, of life with God for the world. That claim is connected to two related claims about the situation in which the church finds itself. The first is simply this: people are thirsty. Deep spiritual thirst—for identity, meaning, security and wholeness—is an inescapable part of the human condition. This deep thirst seems particularly apparent in contemporary Western culture's current fascination with "spirituality." If you visit your local bookstore (if you can still find one with bricks and mortar), you'll find shelves full to overflowing with books on metaphysics, self-help and a whole host of spiritualities—Eastern and Western, old and new. From the sublime to the bizarre, from the ancient to the novel, you'll find more spirituality than you'll know what to do with.

Much has been made of late of the so-called "rise of the nones."[2] A recent study by the Pew Research Religion and Public Life Project identified "nones" as those people with no particular religious affiliation. The Pew research showed that their numbers have been steadily rising in recent years—so much so that Protestant Christians no longer represent the cultural majority in the United States. An increasing number of people in North America now identify themselves as "spiritual but not religious." Many are searching, without the moorings of church and tradition, for something to satiate their deep spiritual thirst.

The second claim that informs this book is that the popular version of Christian piety characterizing much of American Christianity is ill-suited to satisfy the deep thirst so many people are feeling today. Christian spirituality is not doing particularly well in the spiritual marketplace. In the minds of many, it has been tried and found wanting. But could this be true because Christians in North America have presented a fundamentally flawed vision of what Christian spirituality actually is? Could it be that we have reduced Christian spirituality to a narrow set of beliefs and a seemingly restrictive set of moral rules? Moreover, could it be that even our beliefs and morality have been displaced (at least in the minds of many) by other considerations such as zealous nationalism, partisan politics and an adversarial pursuit of cultural power?

Some are beginning to take notice of how these other considerations contribute to Christianity's increasing failure to provide a compelling alternative to the popular cultural conceptions of "the good life." They are beginning to recognize the disastrous effects of this compromised version of Christianity not only on attempts to reach those outside the Christian faith, but even on efforts to pass the Christian faith along to the next generation. The statistics concerning the number of evangelical young people who walk away from their faith after they graduate from high school and leave home are alarming, to say the least.[3] These trends have potentially dire consequences for the future of the church in North America. In his book *The Next Christians*, Gabe Lyons attempts to help the church to name what ails it and to chart a course toward a better future. He writes:

> I believe this moment is unlike any other time in history. Its uniqueness demands an original response. If we fail to offer a

different way forward, we risk losing entire generations to apathy and cynicism. Our friends will continue to drift away, meeting their need for spiritual transcendence through other forms of worship and commitments of faith that may be less true but more authentic and appealing.[4]

One crucial aspect of the task of offering an "original response" to the present crisis is the recovery of a robust vision of Christian spirituality, a spirituality deeply informed by the logic of the incarnation. To be clear, I am not advocating such a view because I take it to be a more "marketable" approach to Christian spirituality or a more effective "strategy" to reach lost people in the kind of world in which we live. I'm advocating it because I believe it captures the essence of the biblical vision of what it means to be fully human. But if that is the case, it is critical for us to recover if we hope to correct the errors of the past and offer a more compelling way forward.

Missional Spirituality/Spiritual Missionality

So what I am advocating in this book is a "missional spirituality" or, if you prefer, a "spiritual missionality." Insisting that these two go together like breathing in and breathing out helps us overcome the potential pathologies associated with both spirituality and missionality. The ancient myths of Narcissus and Prometheus parallel the pathologies toward which both spirituality and missionality can tend. The myth of Narcissus tells the story of an exceptionally handsome and conspicuously proud young woodsman who is lured by Nemesis, the spirit of divine retribution, to a pool where he sees his own reflection and falls in love with it. Consumed by the beauty of his own face, he cannot look away and is doomed to live out the rest of his life fixated on his own image. The story of Prometheus, on the other hand, tells of a Titan of great strength and ingenuity who steals fire from the gods to give to humanity, enabling the progress of human civilization. His actions outrage Zeus, who sentences him to eternal torment. In the classical tradition, the story of Prometheus came to be associated with human striving and the danger of overreaching our limitations.[5]

Narcissistic spirituality. Spirituality, with its emphasis on "the attention we give to our souls,"[6] can easily devolve into a form of narcissism. The attentiveness to the interior life characteristic of many approaches to spirituality can easily lead to self-absorption. As David Augsburger has suggested, "In much contemporary usage, spirituality is a path of self-discovery. It is the secret of releasing and unfolding a deeper, wider, richer, gentler self. It promises, 'You can be the you you long to be.'"[7] As Augsburger's observation makes clear, many contemporary expressions of spirituality are ultimately oriented toward the self. The contemporary cultural environment in which such spirituality is pursued only exacerbates this narcissistic tendency.

Social observers Jean Twenge and Keith Campbell studied the results of 16,275 college students who took the Narcissistic Personality Inventory between 1979 and 2006 and found a rapidly advancing upswing in narcissistic traits over the span of those nearly thirty years. "By 2006, two-thirds of college students scored above the scale's original 1979-85 sample average, a 30% increase in only two decades. One out of 4 recent college students answered the majority of questions in the narcissistic direction."[8] They go on to point out, "The upswing in narcissism appears to be accelerating: the increase between 2000 and 2006 was especially steep."[9] According to Twenge and Campbell, Americans now suffer from narcissistic tendencies in epidemic proportions:

> American culture's focus on self-admiration has caused a flight from reality to the land of grandiose fantasy. We have phony rich people (with interest-only mortgages and piles of debt), phony beauty (with plastic surgery and cosmetic procedures), phony athletes (with performance-enhancing drugs), phony celebrities

(via reality TV and YouTube), phony genius students (with grade inflation), a phony national economy (with $11 trillion of government debt), phony feelings of being special among children (with parenting and education focused on self-esteem), and phony friends (with the social networking explosion). All of this fantasy might feel good, but, unfortunately, reality always wins.[10]

The upswing in narcissistic tendencies in our cultural environment, along with its impact on spirituality, is closely connected to what sociologist and cultural critic Philip Rieff identified in 1966 as "the triumph of the therapeutic."[11] Christopher Lasch, one of Rieff's disciples, captured the sentiment well, saying, "The contemporary climate is therapeutic, not religious. People today hunger not for personal salvation, let alone for the restoration of an earlier golden age, but for the feeling, the momentary illusion, of personal well-being, health, and psychic security."[12] This impassioned pursuit of a sense of personal well-being—which has only grown in the decades since Rieff identified it—has become, for many, the "chief end of man," pursued as an end in itself rather than experienced as the byproduct of some higher end beyond the self.

This cultural trend has not gone without effect on Christian conceptions of spirituality. On the one hand, we can easily veer off into a spirituality in and for the self. By this I have in mind those forms of Christian spirituality that focus primarily on the pursuit of personal wholeness. Much of the popular literature on spirituality tends toward this end; personal well-being, authentic personhood and deep connection with God become the goals we pursue. This type of spirituality tends to focus on the practices an individual can engage in in order to experience the divine and discover one's true self. This approach to the spiritual life emphasizes inwardness, often giving prominence to those spiritual disciplines that involve withdrawal from the chaos of life in the world and retreat into the quiet repose of the presence of God.

My purpose here is not to denigrate the importance of such practices but to point to the ways in which they can devolve into a spiritually sanctioned form of narcissism. Many popular expressions of spirituality today are deeply self-referential, aimed as they are at greater self-awareness, self-actualization and self-fulfillment. As Eugene Peterson has thoughtfully observed, "Spirituality is always in danger of self-absorption, of becoming so intrigued with matters of soul that God is treated as a mere accessory to my experience."[13] When God becomes a mere accessory to my own spiritual experience, his image bearers also fade from my view apart from the degree to which they serve or impede my personal pursuits. The quest for wholeness displaces the quest for God and the love of neighbor.

On the other hand, Christian spirituality can also be reduced to a spirituality in and for the church. Here I am thinking of those forms of popular Christian piety that focus primarily on personal holiness. Our focus all too easily shifts to a kind of negative spirituality, intended to provide us with the resources to avoid the influence of the world. The emphasis here is on what one needs to know and how one needs to act in order to be less encumbered by the beliefs, values and practices of the dominant culture. The world is seen as corrupt and corrupting, so discipleship becomes about evading this corrupting influence. Spirituality becomes primarily about behavior modification—in Dallas Willard's words, about "sin management"—so that we can live more pure and undefiled lives unstained by the world. This approach can reduce spiritual maturity to simply sinning less (or, in its most dangerous form, simply appearing to sin less). Often this approach to the spiritual life presents the church as the place where one finds the resources to live a holy life. Participation in the community of faith and conformity to its behavioral standards become the hallmarks of spiritual life.

Once again, I do not want to diminish the significance of the church for authentic Christian spirituality. My point is simply to name the reality that often characterizes evangelical popular piety. We can live out our Christian lives in an ecclesial bubble, hermetically sealed off from the corrupt and corrupting influence of the world. We may feel better about our lives, our families and our churches, but we will have betrayed our calling in the name of personal holiness.

Of course, the quest for wholeness and holiness are legitimate pursuits. Patterns of growth in wholeness and holiness are vital to any robust vision of Christian spirituality. What I am suggesting is that when these emphases are elevated to the place of prominence that they sometimes receive, the result can be a truncated vision of Christian spirituality, one that is more concerned with getting us out of the world and the world out of us rather than leading us into the world for the sake of the world. As David Gushee has so aptly said,

> A socially disengaged spirituality . . . is inconceivable and inexcusable. Just me and Jesus, growing closer all the time, while the world suffers outside of my field of vision, is a way of being Christian that can flow only from cloistered privilege—or perhaps in some cases from such extraordinary personal misery that an inward spiritual retreat is the only path to emotional survival. I fear that in evangelical Christianity these two paths to mere inwardness sometimes converge—the cloistered privileged ones welcome the personally miserable ones and together they (we) escape the world in the name of Jesus.[14]

To escape the world in Jesus' name is to fail to allow our spirituality to be sufficiently informed by the logic of the incarnation. Christian spirituality in the way of Jesus ought instead to be a spirituality in and for the world.

Promethean missionality. At the same time, missionality can carry its own pathologies. Missionality that is not appropriately spiritual can degenerate into mere activism. When we engage in mission without a deep sense of connection with and dependence on God, our efforts become Promethean self-assertion and accomplishment. The downfall of both Narcissus and Prometheus was ultimately an exaggerated focus on the self. The "inward turn" can affect missional Christians when the mission of God takes the place of God himself and our participation in that mission becomes central to our sense of identity and value. Gordon MacDonald has identified this persistent temptation among more missionally minded Christians as "missionalism." Missionalism involves "the belief that the worth of one's life is determined by the achievement of a grand objective."[15] As MacDonald makes clear, missionalism is in the end a form of idolatry. Our participation in God's mission displaces our trust of, dependence on and delight in God himself.

In a much-discussed blog post, Anthony Bradley scathingly criticized advocates of a missional approach to the Christian faith as the proponents of a "new legalism." Bradley writes,

> I continue to be amazed by the number of youth and young adults who are stressed and burnt out from the regular shaming and feelings of inadequacy if they happen to not be doing something unique and special. Today's millennial generation is being fed the message that if they don't do something extraordinary in this life they are wasting their gifts and potential. The sad result is that so many young adults feel ashamed if they "settle" into ordinary jobs, get married early and start families. . . . For too many millennials their greatest fear in this life is being an ordinary person with a non-glamorous job, living in the suburbs, and having nothing spectacular to boast about.[16]

I believe that Bradley's post is significantly wide of the mark in its criticisms in a number of ways, but the concern that he is raising is not completely unfounded. The call to be unique, special or extraordinary is not what the best advocates of a missional framework for life and faith are saying. Many of my friends who are leaders in the missional church movement do not recognize themselves or their teaching in Bradley's caricature. But it's worth noting that what Bradley is saying is, evidently, what some people are hearing. Any call to activism has the potential to sound like a new legalism. That threat should not cause us to abandon the call to activism, but it should come as a challenge to make sure our profoundly important call to missionality does not devolve into a Promethean missionalism and that in our activism we do not fail to attend to God and to our souls.

One place where the tendency toward a kind of Promethean overreaching shows itself is in the ways we sometimes talk about the kingdom of God. Throughout the literature on what it means to be missional there is an intimate connection between the *missio Dei* and the *regnum Dei*, between the mission of God and the reign of God. To be missional is to have one's life oriented toward the reign of God in the world. With Jesus' incarnation came the inbreaking of the kingdom of God into the dominion of sin, death and the devil. We live now in the overlap of kingdoms. According to the Christian story, there is coming a day when God's kingdom will come in its fullness and when his reign will be uncontested. In that day, everything wrong will be made right, everything broken will be made whole, and everything marred will be made beautiful.

As Darrell Guder and his colleagues noted in *The Missional Church*, things get off track when the church begins to speak of "building" or "extending" the kingdom of God.[17] Such language puts the emphasis on our efforts. On the one hand, talk of "building," "establishing" or "bringing about" the kingdom reduces the reign of God to a social project that we are left to design and implement through our own efforts and ingenuity. Such language overestimates our strength and competence and underestimates the realities of brokenness and injustice in the world. It betrays a distinctly modern hubris foreign to the biblical vision of God's reign.

On the other hand, to speak in terms of "extending," "growing" or "expanding" the kingdom of God can tend toward a reductionism that makes the reign of God merely a spiritual reality entered through repentance and faith. Here the kingdom of God becomes synonymous with eternal life conceived of as the hope of heaven after death. Thus, "extending" or "expanding" the kingdom of God becomes code language for intensifying our efforts in evangelism. Here the emphasis shifts from our herculean strength to our effective strategy. The same modern hubris shows up in the confidence we place in evangelistic techniques and technologies. Evangelism gets reduced to a sales pitch dislocated from the embodied witness of the evangelist and the corporate life of the community of faith. Such a way of thinking and talking about the kingdom makes far too little of what the reign of God actually is and far too much of what our strategies can achieve. Both ways of speaking—whether we talk of "building" or "expanding"—tend to focus the attention on us and our efforts rather than the God whose reign it is. This is the Promethean pathology of missionality.

Vision, Practice and Context

There are three crucial aspects of learning to live the missional spirituality—the life with God for the world—that I am advocating: vision, practice and context. In this book, chapters one through four will focus on the vision of life with God for the world. In his book *Desiring the Kingdom* philosopher James K. A. Smith argues that human beings are teleological creatures. We make our way in the world according to a certain *teleos*, a specific vision of human flourishing that captivates our affections and imagination. He writes, "Our ultimate love is oriented by and to a picture of what we think it looks like for us to live well, and that picture then governs, shapes, and motivates our decisions and actions."[18] That vision takes hold in our lives through the stories and models through which it is conveyed. For us to live out a spirituality informed by the logic of the incarnation, we need to explore in detail the vision this way of life calls us to live. These chapters seek to lay out "the vision of God" that gives rise to the incarnation, that guided the incarnate life of Christ and that ought to deeply shape our understanding of Christian spirituality.

Chapters five through nine will talk about the practices that shape and sustain life with God for the world. Importantly, Christian spirituality is not merely something to be understood but something to be lived. Learning to live into the vision involves our participation in a set of embodied practices. According to Craig Dykstra, "A practice is an ongoing, shared activity of a community of people that partly defines and partly makes them who they are."[19] A certain set of practices has defined and formed the church throughout its history. These practices are not the means by which we transform ourselves, but the "means of grace," the means by which we pay attention to the Spirit's presence and open ourselves up to the Spirit's transformative work. It is only the Spirit's work that brings genuine transformation in the Christian life.

But progress in spiritual formation does not come by accident or chance. As John Stott has said, "Holiness is not a condition into which we drift."[20] The Spirit's transforming power is available to us all and comes to us only as a gift. But we have a responsibility to receive that gift, to allow the Spirit to accomplish his purposes in our lives. The Spirit accomplishes his work in us through appointed means, the historical practices of Christian spirituality. In these chapters I will give attention to a "grammar of the disciplines" that ought to characterize the ways we understand and engage the practice of any of the spiritual disciplines, and I will give extended treatment to a handful of selected disciplines that are crucial for us to recover today in our efforts to live into the vision of God.

Finally, living into this vision of life with God for the world requires us to think about context. The "spiritual life" ought never to be isolated from "the rest of life." This way of thinking leads to a construal of spirituality that is primarily about withdrawal, a kind of spiritual recharge before going out into the world again. Missiologist David Bosch describes the mistake of this way of thinking by saying,

> In this view, then, my "true" Christian life consists of those so-called spiritual moments, away from the hustle and bustle of ordinary life. To be sure, all that hubbub is actually anti-spiritual, because it taps my stored-up spiritual resources, it drains my spiritual power away, it is a threat to my spirituality. I would, therefore, much rather live on angels' food only and have as little as possible to do with the things of this world.[21]

Bosch goes on to articulate a spirituality of engagement that is "all-pervasive," saying, "The involvement in this world should lead to the deepening of our relationship with and dependence on God, and the deepening of this relationship should lead to increasing involvement in the world." The final chapter of the book, then, will explore the contexts in which this involvement is pursued.

The early Christian theologian Irenaeus of Lyon once wrote, "The glory of God is man fully alive."[22] Jesus is the fully human one who came to bring us life and to show us how to live. As we learn to follow the pattern he left for us—life with God for the world—we learn what it means to become fully alive. We find our stories wrapped up in his story.

1

The Stories We Live and the Stories We Live Into

Biblical Narrative and the Vision of God

Man is in his actions and practice, as well in his fictions, essentially a story-telling animal. . . . I can only answer the question "What am I to do?" if I can answer the prior question "Of what story or stories do I find myself a part?"

ALASDAIR MacINTYRE

We carry inside us a vision of wholeness that we sense is our true home and it beckons us.

FREDERICK BUECHNER

Salvation is the delightful surprise of having your little life caught up in the purposes of God for the whole world.

STANLEY HAUERWAS AND WILLIAM WILLIMON

There's a tree-lined path that cuts through the woods behind Magdalen College in Oxford, England. It's called Addison's Walk, named after a fellow at the college during the early eighteenth century. It winds along the edge of the River Cherwell on one side and a picturesque meadow filled with grazing deer on the other. I walked the path a year ago and imagined a conversation that happened there in 1931 between two of the most beloved Christian storytellers of the twentieth century: C. S. Lewis and J. R. R. Tolkien. The two men, along with their friend Hugo Dyson, strolled the path and talked about their shared love of stories, a love that deeply shaped each of their lives as authors and Oxford literature professors. As they walked, Dyson and Tolkien sought to persuade Lewis that the stories they loved were all, in fact, pointers to the story that's true. They suggested that the universal longings embedded in the great myths of the world were met in history in the incarnation. A few days later, in a letter to his boyhood friend Arthur Greeves, Lewis wrote, "I have just passed on from believing in God to definitely believing in Christ—in Christianity. . . . My long night talk with Dyson and Tolkien had a good deal to do with it."[1]

Human beings are relentless storytellers. Our stories allow us to make sense of our lives. They are the means by which we conquer chaos and make meaning. Through stories we fashion a conception of our own identity and form meaningful connections with others. We connect scenes, trace patterns and discover plots in order to bring order to what would otherwise be a random assemblage of one thing after another.

All of us are deeply shaped by two kinds of stories: the stories we live and the stories we live into. The stories we live are our own unique biographies, the collection of experiences, relationships, joys and sorrows that make us who we are. We live out the episodes of life in the ebb and flow of the meaningful and the mundane. And as Gregory Mobley has said, "Each story leads to another as our minds seek to interpret, connect, and harmonize each new story into that single masterpiece we all author, consciousness's magnum opus, every soul's work, the Song of Myself."[2]

But every human being also lives into some larger story, some vision of "the good life" that orients the way we understand who we are and how we get on in the world. These stories precede us and continue beyond us. But they give our lives coherence and direction in the meantime as well. The stories we inhabit shape our values, our decisions and our way of engaging the world. They influence what we love, what we hate, what we do and who we are. As James K. A. Smith has suggested, "We are by nature traditioned creatures who properly find our identity only by being traditioned well."[3] To be "traditioned well" means, at least in part, learning to live into the story of the community of which we are a part.

Christian spirituality (like every other version of spirituality) takes its shape from a particular story. In the case of Christian spirituality, it is the story told in the pages of the Bible and lived out in the history of the church. The Christian story claims to be the true story of God and the world. It claims to be the truest story of what it means to be human, the story that makes the most sense of the reality we bump up against. It's the story that tells us how best to live in this God-made, sin-scarred world. It's the story that tells us where we've come from, where we're going and how to navigate the space between. This navigating the space between is the essence of Christian spirituality. It's not about the pursuit of an esoteric spiritual experience or some celestial encounter with transcendence. It's about life—all of life—lived with and for God in and for the world. It's about learning to live a fully human life now in anticipation of where the story ends. As Eugene Peterson suggests, Christian spirituality "does not present us with a moral code and tell us, 'Live up to this'; nor does it set out a system of doctrine and say, 'Think like this and you will live well.'" Instead, the way of Christian formation is to tell a story and in the telling to invite the hearer, "Live into this—this is what it looks like to be human in this God-made and God-ruled world; this is what is involved in becoming and maturing as a human being."[4]

The purpose of this chapter is to explore what is involved in maturing as a human being by examining the story of God and humanity as told in the Bible. As I've suggested in the introduction, Christian spirituality is fundamentally about becoming like Jesus through the power of the Spirit. But the story of Jesus is incoherent without its backstory. Jesus emerges on the scene in the middle of a much larger narrative. The story Jesus lived makes sense only within the larger story he lived into.

A spirituality deeply informed by the logic of the incarnation involves more than just following the model lived by Jesus. It means learning to live into the larger biblical vision that the incarnation sought to realize, the vision that guided the incarnate life of Jesus himself. To articulate that vision I'd like to highlight three themes that are woven like threads throughout the entire biblical narrative but that come together profoundly in the Incarnation. These three themes together make up what I will refer to as "the biblical vision" or "the vision of God."

The *Visio Dei*

A vision is the perception of an as-yet-unrealized future that captivates the imagination and draws us forward toward its realization. As theologian Gabriel Fackre puts it, "Vision is picturing with the eye of the mind a desirable future state of affairs. It projects on the screen of the future a day when the wolf and the lamb will lie down together. A vision is an imaginative leap into the Not Yet, an internal perception of a scene of fulfillment often portrayed in rich metaphor."[5] What I'm suggesting here is that God has a vision of just such an as-yet-unrealized future toward which all creation moves. This vision is unveiled in the biblical account of creation in the first two chapters of the Bible, Genesis 1–2, and strikingly depicted through those biblical texts that anticipate creation's glorious renewal, most notably in the final two chapters of the Bible, Revelation 21–22. In this sense, we might say the *visio Dei* is the vision that the *missio Dei* seeks to realize. God's action in history, most notably in the incarnation, has been for the purpose of realizing this vision. God's purposeful engagement in the world and our active participation in his work moves all creation toward the realization of a vision that entails three distinct but interconnected emphases: God's personal presence, God's just reign and God's perfect peace.

First, the vision of God is intimately connected to God's personal presence. Richard Foster has suggested that "the unity of the Bible is discovered in the development of life with God as a reality on earth, centered in the person of Jesus."[6] The Bible makes it clear that God's dwelling place is in heaven and ours is here on earth. But what is equally clear is that these two spheres are not separated by some great, unbridgeable chasm. Time and again throughout the biblical story, heaven and earth "overlap and interlock"[7] in such a way that God's presence enters our place. As we will discuss further, God's personal presence with his people is both the great theme and the great problem of the biblical narrative. In the incarnation, the personal presence of God is embodied in Jesus Christ. In his incarnate work, Jesus secured our hope for a coming day when creation will be remade and God will fully and finally make his dwelling place among the people.

A second biblical theme that is central to the vision of God is God's just reign. The creation account in Genesis makes explicitly clear that God is the sovereign creator over all that is. The cosmos rightfully belongs to him and him alone. In that account, we're told that God created human beings as his image bearers to represent his rule over the world. He gives them the task of exercising dominion on his behalf. But in their act of cosmic rebellion, the first human pair subvert God's reign and, in essence, hand the dominion granted to them over to sin, death and the devil. The cosmos becomes contested territory. In the incarnation, God enters the fray of the created order by taking on flesh to reclaim what was rightfully his and to conquer the powers of sin and death. Jesus' first words in the Gospel of Mark are, "The time has come. The kingdom of God has come near. Repent and believe the good news" (Mark 1:15).

A third theme woven throughout the biblical story is the establishment of God's perfect peace. The Hebrew prophets spoke of a day when all that was wrong with the world would be made right and all that was broken with the world would be made whole. They described that day in vivid imagery and captivating metaphor, but they consistently characterized it with the use of a single Hebrew word, the word *shalom. Shalom* is often translated in our English Bibles as the word "peace." But it means much more than our common conceptions of that word convey. Shalom is more than the absence of hostility or an inner sense of personal well-being. The nuances contained in this single Hebrew word require a cluster of English terms to adequately represent it: wholeness, harmony, flourishing, delight, fulfillment. It is closely associated with corresponding terms such as justice and righteousness.

Old Testament scholar Walter Brueggemann suggests that the term "bears tremendous freight—the freight of a dream of God that resists all our tendencies to division, hostility, fear, drivenness, and misery."[8] Shalom is the condition of everything being in accord with God's intentions, everything being "the way it's supposed to be."[9] Shalom is the dream of God for a world set right. It is that state of affairs that results when God's personal presence and just rule are fully realized. The incarnation of Jesus was the incursion of shalom into the brokenness of the world to secure for that world a hope beyond the brokenness.

Knowing the End from the Beginning

My wife and I can hardly watch a movie together if it's one that I've seen and she hasn't. If she knows I know the ending, she'll desperately want me to tell her how things turn out. I, on the other hand, would never want to know the ending prematurely and therefore hold out on her as long as I can. I want her to live through the drama, to feel the tension and suspense. She, however, wants to have the security of knowing that everything turns out okay. (And if it doesn't turn out okay, I'd better not let her start watching it in the first place. She's not much for those movies.)

But sometimes knowing the end of the story from the beginning provides a depth of meaning and understanding that you might not grasp otherwise. One example that comes to mind is M. Night Shyamalan's 1999 film *The Sixth Sense*. The final scene in the film provides a perspective that changes the viewer's understanding of everything that has happened up until that point.

I believe there is something similar at play in the Bible. The final scene of the biblical drama not only gives us the assurance that everything turns out okay but also provides important perspective on everything that has come before. I believe if we understand where the story ends and allow that picture to captivate our imaginations, we will be transformed. As Dietrich Bonhoeffer has said, "The Church of Christ bears witness to the end of all things. It lives from the end, it thinks from the end, it acts from the end, it proclaims its message from the end."[10] The Bible—with all its richness and diversity—is one long, sprawling story of God who seeks to dwell with humanity, to rule over creation and establish his perfect peace.

The biblical narrative finds its consummation in Revelation 21 and 22, the closing scene of the entire story. There John describes a vision of "a new heaven and a new earth" (Revelation 21:1). His language harkens back to that of the Old Testament prophet Isaiah who used the same phrase to speak of a day when the world would be so transformed it would seem entirely remade (Isaiah 65:17; 66:22).[11] Then John says he sees "the Holy City, the New Jerusalem, coming down out of heaven from God" (Revelation 21:2). Again, John's language calls to mind images painted by the words of the Old Testament prophets (Isaiah, chief among them) who anticipated a future transformed Jerusalem that would greatly exceed anything that had come before and that would be accompanied by a new reality of justice and peace.[12]

And then John pens some of the most poignant words in all of Scripture:

> And I heard a loud voice from the throne saying, "Look! God's dwelling place is now among the people, and he will dwell with them. They will be his people, and God himself will be with them and be their God. He will wipe every tear from their eyes. There will be no more death or mourning or crying or pain, for the old order of things has passed away."
>
> He who was seated on the throne said, "I am making everything new!" (Revelation 21:3-4)

John anticipates a great future day when God will fully and finally make his dwelling place with humanity. This element of the final scene gives crucial perspective on everything that comes before it. Like so many others, I was taught all my life that the goal of the story was to "get people to heaven." But the final scene of the Bible makes it unambiguously clear that the goal is to get heaven here, that the earth may become the place where God and his people dwell together.

I'll never forget my experience a number of years ago singing the old hymn "This Is My Father's World" at the funeral of one of my mentors and the father of one of my dearest friends. I'm sure I'd sung the song before. But I'd never really heard it until that day. I choked back tears as we sang about God's handiwork on display in "the rocks and trees, the skies and seas; his hand the wonders wrought." We sang of birds raising their carols to God and how, indeed, all things "declare their maker's praise." I was struck by how appropriate it was that we sang that song given how much Harry had taught me about seeing and communing with God in the world he had made. Harry had understood more than most what the hymn writer meant when he claimed, "He shines in all that's fair." But when we came to the final verse, the tears flowed freely down my cheeks.

> This is my Father's world: O let me ne'er forget
> That though the wrong seems oft so strong, God is the ruler yet.
> This is my Father's world: the battle is not done.
> Jesus who died will be satisfied, and earth and heaven be one.

Harry was buried only a few yards away from where we had buried my own father not that long before. On that day, "the wrong" of this world seemed strong indeed. I desperately needed the reminder that a day was coming when earth and heaven would be one, when God's dwelling place would be among the people, and he would dwell with us.

Rereading the Beginning in Light of the End

A number of biblical scholars have gone to great lengths to demonstrate that this holy city, this New Jerusalem, is depicted as a new temple, the dwelling place of God that encompasses the whole of the new creation.[13] In his climactic vision, John anticipates a day when all creation will be made new—when earth and heaven will be one—and the entirety of this new creation will become the sanctuary of God, his holy dwelling place. In that day there will be no temple because the whole creation will become a temple permeated with the presence of God. He will be with us.

The significance of this depiction of the end of the biblical story takes on new meaning when we look back to the beginning of the story and find that from the start God was interested in the whole earth becoming a temple in which he would dwell with his image bearers. Many biblical scholars have looked at the account of creation in Genesis 1 and 2 and seen connections between the garden God made for humanity to inhabit and the temple Israel would later build as the dwelling place of God. Old Testament scholar Gordon Wenham argues:

> The garden of Eden is not viewed by the author of Genesis simply as a piece of Mesopotamian farmland, but as an archetypal sanctuary, that is a place where God dwells and where man should worship him. Many of the features of the garden may also be found in later sanctuaries, particularly the tabernacle or Jerusalem temple. These parallels suggest that the garden itself is understood as a sort of sanctuary.[14]

This observation, that the garden of Eden is best seen as a prototypical sanctuary or garden-temple, carries with it important implications for understanding the calling of the man and woman God placed in the garden. After creating them male and female in his image, God commanded them, "Be fruitful and increase in number; fill the earth and subdue it" (Genesis 1:28). God's blueprint for creation was for his image bearers to expand the boundaries of this garden-temple so that it would eventually fill the whole earth. As one biblical scholar puts it, "Adam's purpose in that first garden-temple was to expand its boundaries until it circumscribed the earth, so that the earth would be completely filled with God's glorious presence."[15] From the beginning of the biblical story to its completion, the emphasis lies on God's desire to be with us.

Let Them Rule

There is another enormously important detail in the account of the New Jerusalem in the closing scenes of the biblical narrative. We're told there that the voice John hears saying, "I am making everything new" comes from one who is "seated on the throne" (Revelation 21:5). The throne of God is one of the great recurring images throughout the book of Revelation, but it's not until Revelation 21 that the throne is on earth. John elaborates on this in the opening verses of the next chapter where he writes,

> Then the angel showed me the river of the water of life, as clear
> as crystal, flowing from the throne of God and of the Lamb down
> the middle of the great street of the city. . . . The throne of God
> and of the Lamb will be in the city, and his servants will serve
> him. (Revelation 22:1-3)[16]

In his repeated references to the throne of God in the New Jerusalem,
John depicts a coming day when God renews creation and reigns over
it without hindrance or rival. The great hope of the Bible is not for
disembodied humans to float in the eternal ether of heaven with harps
and angel wings. It is to see the realization of the uninhibited reign of
God over the good creation that he has made.

The idea of God as king is basic to biblical belief. In Psalm 10:16 the
psalmist declares, "The LORD is King forever and ever." He alone is
creation's rightful sovereign. But due to the pervasiveness of rebellion
against God's rule, a number of passages in the Old Testament anticipate a day when God's rightful reign will be fully established and uncontested. The prophet Zechariah wrote of that day, saying, "The
LORD will be king over the whole earth. On that day there will be one
LORD, and his name the only name" (Zechariah 14:9). When the reign
of God comes in its fullness it will overthrow and vanquish all that is
contrary to his righteous rule. Justice will prevail. His will will be done
on earth as it is in heaven. Especially evident in the depictions of the
coming of the just reign of God is the concern "to vindicate God's
sovereignty against any presumptuous power that dares to impose
slavery on any human being, the masterpiece of God's creation."[17]

This observation leads us once again to look at the connection between the creation blueprint and the realization of God's intentions
in the future. Returning to the creation account in Genesis, we find
that the storyteller has constructed the account in ways that ancient
readers would have understood to be deliberately connected to royalty
and dominion, to the reign of God over all creation. The account of

creation in Genesis 1 is a highly stylized, almost liturgical account that
pulses with rhythm and repetition:

> And God said . . . And God said . . . And God said . . .
> Let there be . . . Let there be . . . Let there be . . .
> It was so. . . . It was so. . . . It was so. . . .
> It was good. . . . It was good. . . . It was very good.

The account begins by saying that the earth was "formless and empty"
(Genesis 1:2). Over the course of the first three days, God brings form.
Over the second three days, God fills the emptiness.

The depiction in Genesis 1 stands in contrast to the creation stories
of Israel's neighbors in the ancient Near East. In those stories, creation
emerges from chaos as a result of conflict between the gods. In many
of those stories, the created order is inherently flawed and the forces
of chaos and evil abound. In Israel's story, God creates without ob-
struction or rival by the word of his mouth. He takes delight in what
he has made because it is very good.

The point of the whole account seems to be that it was Israel's God
who did it all. Many of the things God is said to create in Genesis 1 were
worshiped as gods by Israel's neighbors. Genesis 1 sets out to make it
clear that Israel's God is the sovereign creator of everything that exists
and that the whole of creation is the sphere of his divine rule.

In Genesis 1:26, God determines to create human beings as his
image bearers. Once again the contrast between Israel's creation story
and the other ancient creation accounts is striking. In those stories,
the only one created in the image of a god was the king. All other
human beings were created as slaves to serve the gods and the royal
image bearers. In Israel's story, all human beings are created with a
regal dignity unmatched in all of creation. Humans alone are said to
be made in the image of God.

In the ancient Near East, when a king extended his reign into a new
territory he would set up a physical image of himself to indicate that

this territory was under his dominion. Ancient readers would recognize something similar at play in this story when God creates humankind in his image. Then, in Genesis 1:28, the storyteller recounts God's words to his image bearers: "God blessed them and said to them, 'Be fruitful and increase in number; fill the earth and subdue it. Rule over the fish in the sea and the birds in the sky and over every living creature that moves on the ground.'" Adam and Eve are created to bear the image of God by representing his reign over creation and exercising dominion on his behalf. They are commissioned as vice regents on behalf of the rightful king of creation. Their task is to ensure that God's will is done on earth as it is in heaven.

When we come to Genesis 2, the storyteller backs up and narrates the events of creation again, this time emphasizing the creation of Adam from the ground. In the Genesis account of things, God handcrafts the archetypal human body from the dust of the earth. It is an act of a potter shaping his clay, a work of art in accord with the artist's design. The human body is a beautiful expression of divine ingenuity. Contrary to the dualistic assumptions that have too often crept into Christian theology, the human body is not a thing of shame and disgrace, a bondage from which we seek liberation. Having a body is fundamental to what it means to be human. It is a part of God's good creation.

In addition to God's work of formation, Genesis depicts God undertaking an intimate act of animation, breathing his life-giving breath into the nostrils of the body he has formed (Genesis 2:7). With this act God unites flesh and spirit, soul and body. It is worth noting that in both the Hebrew of the Old Testament and the Greek of the New Testament, the word for "breath" and "spirit" are the same. In Genesis, the physical body and the animating spirit are integrally related—a person is not whole without both. In the biblical story, human beings are not fundamentally souls who happen to have bodies. As Dietrich Bonhoeffer has said of the first man, "His body belongs to his essential being. Man's body is not his prison, his shell, his exterior, but man himself. Man does not 'have' a body; he does not 'have' a soul; rather he 'is' body and soul."[18]

In both the first two chapters and the last two chapters of the Bible, we find pictorial depictions of the way things are meant to be. In both places we find God's uninhibited reign in and over the entirety of his creation. In both places we find God's embodied image bearers living with him under sovereign care.

All Manner of Things Shall Be Well

The story we live into in Christian spirituality is the great narrative of Scripture stretched between the garden-temple of Genesis and the temple-city of Revelation. In both the garden and the city—the dwelling place of God and the dwelling place of humanity—heaven and earth "overlap and interlock." Everything is in its right place. Everything is "the way it's supposed to be." John the Seer captures this with a tender image: "He will wipe every tear from their eyes. There will be no more death or mourning or crying or pain, for the old order of things has passed away" (Revelation 21:4).

The "old order of things"—the world as we now know it—is characterized by heartache, loss, grief and pain. The new world will be characterized by comfort, joy and perfect peace—the shalom of God. The words John records in Revelation echo the poetry of the prophet Isaiah, who penned words of hope in the midst of the old order of things at its worst. He wrote of the coming day of a great banquet on Mt. Zion:

> On this mountain the LORD Almighty will prepare
>   a feast of rich food for all peoples,
> a banquet of aged wine—
>   the best of meats and the finest of wines.
> On this mountain he will destroy

the shroud that enfolds all peoples,
the sheet that covers all nations;
   he will swallow up death forever.
The Sovereign LORD will wipe away the tears
   from all faces;
he will remove his people's disgrace
   from all the earth.
      The LORD has spoken. (Isaiah 25:6-8)

Isaiah's vision of a great feast captures the theme of shalom that reverberates throughout the biblical narrative: the dream of God for a world set right. The prophets describe it as a day when "the wolf will live with the lamb" (Isaiah 11:6), when former enemies will "beat their swords into plowshares and their spears into pruning hooks" (Isaiah 2:4), when "new wine will drip from the mountains and flow from all the hills" (Amos 9:13), and when "the earth will be filled with the knowledge of the glory of the LORD as the waters cover the sea" (Habakkuk 2:14).

Shalom is an inescapably relational term. It is the webbing together of all creation in wholeness, harmony and flourishing. Nicholas Wolterstorff captures the relational dimensions of the word when he writes, "Shalom is the human being dwelling at peace in all his or her relationships: with God, with self, with fellows, with nature."[19]

Perhaps nothing in the Genesis account captures the essence of shalom more than the depiction of God's Sabbath rest on the seventh day. The great German theologian Helmut Thielicke describes the scene poetically:

Heaven and earth and all its hosts are now complete. And as the young world in all its dewy freshness exults in the surge of life— the whales romping in the sea, the trees blooming and fading, the stars circling in their courses, and man roaming through the Garden of Eden—the Creator withdraws into a solemn, cele-

brative stillness. . . . On the border between the completed work
of creation and the noisy alarms of history there is a great silence,
the resting hush of the Creator.[20]

The seventh day—the divine Sabbath—is the day in which God rests
to delight in the flourishing of his good creation. Everything is in its
right place. Thus, the rest of God on the seventh day of creation anticipates the dream of God realized in the new creation. Thielicke
writes, "The gaze of the church has always passed from this sabbath
after the completion of the work of creation to the last day of the world
when the sabbath of eternity will conclude and resolve the restlessness
of history."[21]

Pulling It All Together

This examination of God's blueprint in the garden and its realization
in the new heavens and new earth allows us to draw some general
conclusions about what God is up to between the garden and the city,
which includes not only the rest of the biblical narrative but also what
he's doing in our own day. The rest of the story from the garden to
the city is the story of the mission of God to rescue and renew his
good but broken creation so that he might dwell with humanity and
reign over creation in perfect peace. This is the story that gives
Christian spirituality its distinctive shape. This is the story we're
learning to live into. There is, quite obviously, more to be said about
the story. A lot happens between the garden and the city. But we're
in a position at this point to draw six fundamentally important conclusions about Christian spirituality that will be developed further in
the subsequent chapters.

First, Christian spirituality is creation affirming. As the old hymn
states, "This is my Father's world. He shines in all that's fair." And as
the final line of the song insists, the Christian hope is that one day
earth and heaven will finally be one. In the beginning God looked at

what he had made and said, "It is very good." He is not interested in scrapping his work. And our hope is not to escape this place. The goal of the story is not to get to heaven. The goal is for God to bring heaven here. That means that Christian spirituality should take great concern to delight in and care for God's good but broken creation. And we should develop eyes to see the myriad ways in which "he shines in all that's fair." A sumptuous meal, a breathtaking sunset or the sounds of a bird raising its carol to its maker are all tokens of God's love for us and all creation.

Second, Christian spirituality is people affirming. As the Christian story goes, human beings were not created to be slaves of the gods but to bear the image of the one true God. As such, human beings have an unmatched dignity in all of creation. In the ancient world it was understood that if you defiled the image of a god you were acting directly against that god itself. What you did to the image you did to the god.[22] This principle applies equally well to the images of the God of the Bible. To mistreat, exploit or dishonor a human being—any human being—is a direct affront to the God who made people and whose image they bear. Christian spirituality should never be reduced to a two-dimensional relationship between an individual and God. Christian spirituality is inherently related to how we relate to other people. We cannot honor God if we do not honor people. We cannot love God if we do not love people. We cannot obey the first great commandment and not obey the second. They are fundamentally and inextricably interconnected. Thus, Christian spirituality is inherently relational. It is not about "me and my God" but about "us and our God." This has a host of implications concerning our "near neighbors" and our "far neighbors" that will be developed as we move forward.

Third, Christian spirituality is body affirming. God created his image bearers as embodied creatures who can experience his presence and delight in his creation. Our hope is not that we will escape our bodies and spend eternity as incorporeal spirits floating in the clouds.

From the garden to the city—from creation to the new creation—Christian spirituality esteems the body. The Christian hope in a new heaven and a new earth is accompanied by the hope of a new resurrected body. According to the apostle Paul, these bodies of ours that decay and die will one day be "raised imperishable," "raised in glory," "raised in power" (1 Corinthians 15:42-43). The Christian hope is an embodied hope. That means for us that Christian spirituality is not something experienced merely in the depths of our being, in the deep recesses of our souls. Christian spirituality is experienced in our bodies. It insists that the formation of the soul is integrally connected to the bodies in which we dwell. Any bifurcation between the spiritual and physical has no place in spirituality that claims the name Christian. "The body is not a tomb but a wondrous masterpiece of God, constituting the essence of man as fully as the soul."[23]

Fourth, Christian spirituality is intimately connected to the presence of God. More remains to be said about experiencing the presence of God between the garden and the city. But as we have seen, the biblical story both begins and ends with God making his dwelling place with humanity in perfect peace. The great theme and the great problem of the biblical narrative is life with God. This theme points us forward to what we'll say in subsequent chapters about the presence of God in the incarnation and the outpouring of the Spirit. But here it can suffice to say that the fully human life—the life we were created for and will one day experience in its fullness—is life lived in the presence of God.

Fifth, our look at the beginning and end of the biblical story allows us to say that Christian spirituality is intimately connected to the just reign of God. Human beings were created with a distinct purpose—to see that God's will is done on earth as it is in heaven. As we live in the time between the old order of things and everything made new, we are to pray that his kingdom would come and we are to shape our lives in accord with what we know is coming. We cannot bring God's reign into the world. We do not "build" his kingdom. It will not come as the result of our ethical accomplishments. But we can live in such a way that points toward and foreshadows what we know God has in store for the world's future. We cannot afford to create a division between spirituality and our concrete action in the world. As Lesslie Newbigin has said, "To make disciples is to call and equip men and women to be signs and agents of God's justice in all human affairs."[24]

Finally, our examination of the stories of creation and consummation remind us that Christian spirituality is about sharing in God's dream of shalom and allowing that dream to pervade our lives. Shalom is the hope to which we cling, the hope that pulls us forward. It is the gift we have been given in measure and will one day be given in fullness. And it is the task to which we have been called as we seek to bring glimpses of the world to come into the world as we know it. As N. T. Wright has said, "We are called to be part of God's new creation, called to be agents of that new creation here and now. We are called to model and display that new creation in symphonies and family life, in restorative justice and poetry, in holiness and service to the poor, in politics and painting."[25] Christian spirituality lives from the end of the story, thinks from the end of the story, prays from the end of the story. It eats, drinks, laughs, loves, struggles, plays and dreams from the end of the story. And as it does, it lives into the story of the vision of God.

Genesis gives us the story's outline; Revelation, its denouement. At the center of the story, between the two, we find the incarnation, the incursion of the presence of God, the reign of God and the shalom of God into the middle of the story. He was "the first wave of the in-breaking future."[26] The world to come invaded the world as we know it. The Word took on flesh and dwelt among us, because the world as we know it got bent and broken.

Bent and Broken

The Vision of God and the Vandalism of Shalom

If we are fully at home in our situation, then we will
not ponder a better tomorrow. Discontent is the mother of invention.
Discontent is holy when it compels us to dream of redemption. . . .
All good grows out of a desire to see the future shaped
from the refuse of the present.

DAN ALLENDER

Ring the bells that still can ring
Forget your perfect offering
There is a crack in everything
That's how the light gets in

LEONARD COHEN

Sacred discontent is the birthplace of missional spirituality. It emerges from a staunch refusal to remain content with our lives as they are in the world as it is. In the previous chapter we considered the vision of God, his blueprint for creation, his personal presence with his image bearers, his just rule over creation and his perfect peace pervading all things. But the world as we know it is a far cry from this original intention.

My friend Trey is a storyteller. He travels the world with his camera to help nonprofit organizations working in some of the most broken places on earth tell their stories of hope and healing to people far away who have the goodwill and the resources to help the work continue. Trey's stories are deeply motivated by his sharing in the dream of God, the dream of shalom. Two of Trey's photographs I've always found particularly arresting, not only because of their beauty and the skill of their composition but also because of the theological significance the images reflect.

The first is a photograph of an enormous statue of Vladimir Lenin taken in Yerevan, Armenia, in the fall of 2010. Trey had heard a rumor that a statue was hidden away in a restricted-access area at the National Gallery. He barely averted an international incident in gaining access and getting the picture. His story behind the photo includes an unfriendly escort from the premises, the confiscation of his camera and the pulling of some high-powered diplomatic strings to get it back.

The statue was erected several decades ago during communist rule. Like the image of a king set up in the ancient Near East, it was meant to be a constant reminder to the people of the ultimate authority under which they lived. But what's so compelling about the photograph is that the statue is not standing tall in majesty; it has been toppled and decapitated, left lying bent, broken and out of sight. It's a picture dripping with irony. The image of majesty and power wielded for contemptible purposes now lies fallen. It no longer represents nobility and dominion. It is instead an object of shame and disgrace.

The second image is of Ravanniah, a man Trey met in a village of makeshift tents outside a small town in India miles away from any place most Westerners have ever heard of, much less visited. Ravanniah spent most his life eking out a living as a rickshaw puller in the

city. But when he discovered white spots on his arms—telltale signs
of the emergence of a form of leprosy that still plagues that part of the
world—he knew the life he had known was over. Ravanniah now lives
as an elder in a colony of people who are considered unclean and
untouchable. Most of the people in this community live there because
leprosy has disfigured them, damaging their nerves and slowly debilitating their bodies. Some are children who have yet to experience the
devastating physical manifestations of the disease but have already
been touched by its dire social consequences. They are castoffs of their
society, physically and socially isolated, robbed of dignity.

As Trey listened to Ravanniah's story he learned of a group of
people who had moved into the village to bring the hope of the gospel
of Jesus into their midst. These people told the story of a God of love
who had entered the brokenness of the world to bring healing and
restoration. And they embodied that kind of love in the village. In so
doing they brought with them glimpses of the world to come. Ravanniah told Trey, with the tears of a grateful heart streaming down his
face, "Leprosy stole my humanity. But one day I will be made new."

These two images—one of a broken statue, the other of a broken
man—each reflect profound truth about the human condition. We are
all bent and broken. The damage done by sin has left us with a bent
toward evil. Made to represent the reign of God on earth, we're now
twisted and distorted, burdened by the weight of shame and regret.
And yet in many ways great and small we persist in our rebellion.
Further, the damage done by sin has left us scarred. Our bodies decay
and die. We contract disease. We suffer from physical pain, from emotional wounds, from betrayal. Blaise Pascal has aptly written, "Man's
greatness and wretchedness are so evident that the true religion must
necessarily teach us that there is in man some great principle of
greatness and some great principle of wretchedness."[1] We are indeed
great because we are image bearers of God. But we are also wretched
because we are broken people living in a broken world.

Everything Comes Apart

Increasingly, the concept of sin has become something of a "snicker word" in our contemporary environment. As sociologist James Davidson Hunter has observed, the only things described as sinful anymore are those things that show up on dessert menus. Sin has become a word used to advertise our guilty pleasures. The character traits ancient monks described as "the seven deadly sins" don't evoke the same grave moral concern they once did. Rather, they seem to have subtly crept into the fabric of our social lives. Pride becomes the key to personal success. Greed, the key to a successful economy. Envy and lust, the keys to a successful marketing campaign. As Neal Plantinga has suggested, "The awareness of sin used to be our shadow. Christians hated it, feared it, fled from it, grieved over it. . . . But the shadow has dimmed. Nowadays, the accusation *you have sinned* is often said with a grin, and with a tone that signals an inside joke."[2]

Christian communities have largely gone one of two ways with regard to the vocabulary of sin. Some have followed the trend of the broader culture and largely eliminated the language of sin from their theological vernacular. In order to be taken seriously by a culture that now finds the concept of sin something of a joke, many people use the language of psychology and self-help rather than the language of the Christian tradition. Others have pursued a different course, becoming the self-appointed moral conscience of the culture and community. They've managed to maintain a serious concept of sin, though they tend to be narrowly focused on personal morality—especially those aspects they find particularly salacious. Rarely do these churches attend to issues of systemic injustice with anywhere near the same passion they display regarding issues of individual ethics. As Richard Rohr has recently observed, this type of Christian community tends to be much more concerned about what people are doing in beds than about whether everyone has a bed to begin with.[3]

An articulation of spirituality that is worthy of the name "Christian" needs a robust account of what's wrong with the world and each of us in it. The realities of shame, betrayal, suffering and injustice are inescapable in the world as we know it. And we lack the capacity to talk about them or deal with them in ways that are distinctly Christian apart from reviving the language of sin. We must avoid the tendency to reduce spirituality to what Dallas Willard called "sin management" and the penchant of some to confuse the quest for spiritual maturity with merely "sinning less than I do right now." What we need in order to live into the Christian story is a richer understanding of how sin has corrupted God's cosmos, subverted God's reign and ravaged God's shalom. A deeper understanding of sin in our lives and the world must inform the way we think about what it means to live life with God for the world and will help us grasp why adopting such a way of life is so difficult.

The Great Rupture

There is a deep sense of discord between what we learn of what it means to be human in God's world from the first and last chapters of the Bible and what we know of humanity in history and experience. This dissonance is not resolved but is made comprehensible by the account of the fall—"the great rupture"—we find in Genesis 3.[4] As Peter Kreeft has said, "What happened in Eden may be hard to understand, but it makes everything else understandable."[5]

In Genesis 3:6 we find what surely must be the most tragic lines any storyteller ever penned: "When the woman saw that the fruit of the tree was good for food and pleasing to the eye, and also desirable for gaining wisdom, she took some and ate it. She also gave some to her husband, who was with her, and he ate it." As the Christian story goes, all the pain and brokenness we experience in this world has its origin in some mysterious way in that first enigmatic act of sedition. Our first parents used their freedom to become a law unto themselves, violating the one prohibition God had placed on their enjoyment of his good creation. And with that act of rebellion, everything comes undone.

When Adam and Eve heed the words of the serpent in Genesis 3, they commit an act of cosmic treason. Not only is God's dwelling place despoiled, but his authority structure is subverted. God's reign over creation is sabotaged. The dominion given to humanity is relinquished. As Desmond Alexander writes, "By betraying God and obeying the serpent, the royal couple dethroned God. . . . The ones through whom God's sovereignty was to be extended throughout the earth side with his enemy. By heeding the serpent they not only give it control over the earth, but they themselves become its subjects."[6] To be sure, God is still the rightful sovereign over his creation, but his sovereignty is contested between the garden and the city. This world that rightfully belongs under the reign of God exists after Eden under the reign of sin, death and the devil.

Everything God's good creation experiences between the beginning of the story and its end—including the time in which we now live—is characterized by the brokenness of sin. Neal Plantinga uses a remarkably suggestive little phrase to capture the essence of sin. According to Plantinga, sin is "the vandalism of shalom." He writes,

> God hates sin not just because it violates his law but, more substantively, because it violates shalom, because it breaks the peace, because it interferes with the way things are supposed to be. . . . God is for shalom and therefore against sin. In fact, we may safely describe evil as any spoiling of shalom, whether physically (e.g., by disease), morally, spiritually, or otherwise.[7]

When sin enters the story, shalom is vandalized. God's glorious intention for his good creation is subverted. The wholeness and harmony we were created to enjoy with God, with each other, with creation and with ourselves is fundamentally violated.

The First Mourning

Some time ago I came across a hauntingly beautiful painting by a

French artist from the late nineteenth century named William-Adolphe Bouguereau. The name of the painting is *The First Mourning*, and it portrays a man and a woman in a barren landscape set against a dark and ominous sky. The man is Adam, seated with a look of anguish on his face and one hand resting on his heart. His other arm is draped over his wife, Eve, who is kneeling beside him with her face buried in her hands, leaning into his chest. Across Adam's lap is the pale corpse of a young man. It's the body of their son, Abel, who has been murdered by his brother Cain. This is "the first mourning" as Adam and Eve discover the lifeless body of their beloved child.

In the image Bouguereau has captured the various reasons we experience the vandalism of shalom. First, we experience the vandalism of shalom because of our own foolish, sinful choices. There is a very real sense in which Adam and Eve are experiencing this moment of torment because of their own sin in the garden. They surely can't help but recognize in that moment that they have some culpability in the death of their son. In the garden they despoiled the peace creation was meant to enjoy, and in doing so they passed on to all their progeny "a biblically certified and empirically demonstrable bias toward evil."[8] Each of us in some measure is complicit in and therefore responsible for the vandalism of shalom.

But Bouguereau's image also reminds us that we experience the vandalism of shalom because of the sin of others over which we have no control. We are broken by what others have done to us. In this moment of great grief, Adam and Eve are suffering at the hands of another. This son of theirs, who as a boy climbed lovingly into his father's lap, now lies there lifeless because of the murderous anger of their firstborn. Like Abel, they have become victims of Cain's rage. And like them, all of us suffer violation and betrayal. Some of us carry deep scars from abuse, infidelity or exploitation. But all of us in one way or another experience the vandalism of shalom that comes from the sin of others.

(Third,) this powerful depiction of the first mourning reminds us that we all experience the vandalism of shalom merely by living in a fallen world, a world where loved ones die and everyone grieves. Mourning becomes an inescapable reality once sin enters the story. Even the portrayal of creation in Bouguereau's painting reminds its viewers that we're no longer in the garden. The ground beneath their feet is barren, desolate. The sky above them is threatening, with dark shades of blue and gray dominating the horizon. There is only one glimmer of light breaking through far off in the distance. The world they (and we) inhabit is broken. The force of this brokenness is felt even more fully in looking at the painting if you know that Bouguereau painted it shortly after the death of one of his own sons. In a fallen world, we all experience the vandalism of shalom.

The World, the Flesh and the Devil ENEMIES

The Christian tradition has long affirmed that there are three primary enemies of the soul—three forces that conspire together against shalom. These vandals are the world, the flesh and the devil. The apostle Paul mentions all three in his depiction of the human condition in the opening verses of Ephesians 2:

> As for you, you were dead in your transgressions and sins, in which you used to live when you followed the ways of this world and the ruler of the kingdom of the air, the spirit who is now at work in those who are disobedient. All of us also lived among them at one time, gratifying the cravings of our flesh and following its desires and thoughts. (Ephesians 2:1-3)

We would do well to understand these enemies of the soul more deeply.

The world. There are two statements in the New Testament (each traditionally attributed to the apostle John) that seem on the surface to be impossible to reconcile. In one of the most well-known passages in all of Scripture we read, "For God so loved the world that he gave his one and only Son, that whoever believes in him shall not perish but have eternal life" (John 3:16). Then in 1 John 2:15 we read, "Do not love the world or anything in the world. If anyone loves the world, the love of the Father is not in them." How can it be that we are expressly forbidden to do the very thing that God himself does—namely, "love the world"? It would be handy at this point if we could say that this was only a problem in English, if we could show that there are two different Greek words at play that point to two different kinds of love or two different entities in view. But no such semantic escape is available to us. In both cases we have *agape* (love) and *cosmos* (world).

It seems to me that what we have here is not so much a contradiction as much as a tension that we ought not be too quick to resolve. On the one hand, the New Testament writers can speak of the cosmos to refer to the entire created order, which is the good creation of God, though subject to the corruption of sin. I remember being a kid in Sunday school and being told I could put my own name in John 3:16—"For God so loved me . . ." While this says something beautiful and true, it also says something different from what the text actually says, because John says that God sent his Son into the cosmos because he loved the cosmos in its entirety. In the previous chapter I argued that Christian spirituality should be creation affirming. This is my Father's cosmos. He shines in all that's fair. That includes all of his creation, every human being and every human culture. God loves the cosmos. Jesus has come to redeem it and will come again to renew it. It is in this sense of the word that I have been advocating a spirituality for the world.

But the statement from John's epistle is a clear indication that the word *cosmos* can function differently in some contexts. In the context of 1 John (as in the Ephesians passage above), the word is being used to refer to the corrupt and corrupting ways in which broken creation and rebellious humanity stand in opposition to God and his purposes. Sin is not only soul sickness but social sickness. It is deeply embedded not only in the human psyche but in every human culture. The world holds out cheap substitutes for shalom. But we find them alluring. Enticed by their charm, we all too easily find ourselves wrapped in the tendrils of "the ways of the world." It is in this sense of the word that the Christian tradition has called the world an enemy of the soul. It is in this sense that Christian tradition has long emphasized a posture of spirituality *against the world*. Walter Brueggemann captures the essence of this posture when he writes, "We are identified as the odd ones in the world, called to be at odds with the world, ordained to call into question the world's ways of doing business."[9]

Lesslie Newbigin calls this approach to spirituality the *"Pilgrim's Progress* model." He writes, "The emphasis is on a decisive break by which the Christian separates himself from this world, flees from the 'wicked city' and makes for his true home in another world. In this model 'the world' is felt primarily as a threat, as a source of contagion from which the Christian must keep himself free."[10] Newbigin contrasts this with the *for the world* posture, which he calls the "Jonah model." Here too there is a "wicked city," but the command of God is not to get out but to go in. Jonah provokes God's anger precisely because he flees the wicked city.

Newbigin suggests that while these two models might seem at first to be fundamentally incompatible, pulling in opposite directions, they both actually have roots in Scripture. Throughout the Bible there is a kind of tension between the two. We frequently try to resolve this tension by striking a fine balance: just so much flight from the world coupled with just so much engagement with the world will make everything run smoothly. But as David Bosch suggests, "This balance may be just a new form of self-deception."[11]

What we need is not a balance between the two. What we need is to learn that a spirituality deeply informed by the logic of the incarnation embraces the tension, lives within it and recognizes that our attempts to resolve it in either direction can be a compromise of faithfulness. It is the incarnate one himself who models what it looks like to live in that tension. He models it throughout his life, but he models it most profoundly in the cross. As Newbigin concludes, "The Cross is in one sense an act of total identification with the world. But in another sense it is an act of radical separation. It is both of these things at the same time."[12] The church's being "called out" and being "sent in" are not two callings but one and the same. We do not have spirituality and mission. We have a missional spirituality. We are called to a way of life that is against the world for the sake of the world.

The flesh. Just we are prone to misunderstand what it means to call the world an "enemy of the soul," so too there is great potential for misconstruing the meaning of "the flesh." The concept of the flesh as an enemy of the soul has its roots in the writing of the apostle Paul. When Paul speaks of "the flesh" he is speaking metaphorically. He is not referring to the body and denigrating the body in comparison to the spiritual aspect of human nature. This is a Platonic conception but decidedly not a biblical one. In his book *Tortured Wonders: Spirituality for People, Not Angels*, Rodney Clapp rightly insists,

> The traditional Christian anthropology—or understanding of personhood—does not succumb to the dualism that glorifies the soul and denigrates the body. The soul as the vitalizer and director of the body no more makes the body unimportant or disposable than does a parent's procreation and direction of offspring make children unimportant or disposable. In Christian spirituality soul and body are integral—no person is whole without both. . . . Orthodox Christian spirituality essentially and necessarily links the formation of the soul and spirit to the givens of the body and to the teaching and formation of the body.[13]

As stated previously, Christian spirituality is body affirming. The incarnation itself is our most glorious reminder that the human body is not inherently corrupt. God took one on to dwell among us.

Then what does Paul mean when he speaks of the flesh? In what sense is the flesh an enemy of the soul? Scot McKnight suggests that we understand Paul's reference to the flesh as a metaphor describing "the total person living outside of God's will and apart from God's guiding influence through the Spirit."[14] The flesh is the outlook oriented toward the self, living in autonomous independence from God.[15]

There is a suggestive little Latin phrase with roots in the theology of St. Augustine that brilliantly captures the essence of what is wrong with human beings in our fallen condition: *homo incurvatus in se*—the being turned in upon himself. In our fallen condition we all suffer from an "incurvature of the soul."[16] Theologian Gabriel Fackre captures this well when he defines sin as "the code word in the Christian Story for the turning inward of the self, and thus the turning away from God, neighbor, and nature." Fackre goes on to say that sin is "the use of our freedom to serve ourselves, rather than the employment of that freedom in the service of God and the divine purpose. Sin is an 'ego-trip' inward, rather than a pilgrimage outward and ahead toward the horizon of Shalom."[17]

If we stop to consider our most persistent struggles with sin, we will find that behind them all is the *homo incurvatus in se*. Behind all our sin is the outlook oriented toward the self. Pride is an exalted view of myself. Envy is a resentment of what another has that is not mine. Wrath is the fury born from not getting things my way. Gluttony claims more than it needs for my satisfaction. Lust exploits another for my pleasure. Greed is insatiable desire aimed at more for me. Sloth is the inordinate desire to maintain my status quo.

According to Jesus the essence of spirituality—of life with God—is learning to love God with all you are and all you have and learning to love your neighbor as yourself. Christian spirituality is about the outward turn, overcoming the incurvature of the soul. The power to overcome the inward turn will not come from within the self. It can come only from the empowering presence of the Holy Spirit. Thus the apostle Paul can say, "You, my brothers and sisters, were called to be free. But do not use your freedom to indulge the flesh; rather, serve one another humbly in love. . . . So I say, walk by the Spirit, and you will not gratify the desires of the flesh" (Galatians 5:13, 16). Learning what it means to walk by the Spirit will be the subject of the next chapter.

The devil. According to the biblical story, there is a will at work in the world that seeks to thwart God's intention and corrupt his good creation in any way possible. But just as sin has become a "snicker word," the idea of the devil has also become trivialized. Images of a comically sinister red man with horns, a pointed tail and a pitchfork have made the devil something of a joke, the holdover of a bygone era that saw the devil behind all sorts of things for which we now have perfectly good, rational explanations. The devil is nothing more than superstitious mumbo-jumbo.

In a classic line from the movie *The Usual Suspects* we're told, "The greatest trick the devil ever pulled was convincing the world he didn't exist." But without an accounting of the reality of metaphysical evil, we are left with purely natural explanations of the evil we encounter in the world. Cruelty and injustice are often explained away through psychology and sociology. But I'm convinced that these natural explanations are insufficient to account for either the depth or breadth—the gratuitous horror or the universal reach—of evil. The better explanation, in my view, is that there is a will at work in the world seeking to thwart God's intention and corrupt his good creation in any way possible.

We're not very threatened by the guy in the red suit and pitchfork. But the devil is more crafty than that. In a brilliant song called "Hell Is Chrome," Jeff Tweedy, the lead singer of Wilco, sings, "When the devil came, he was not red. He was chrome. And he said, 'Come with me.'" The devil knows precisely how to entice creatures turned in upon themselves. In his marvelous book *The Screwtape Letters*, C. S. Lewis masterfully captures the schemes of the devil to exploit the vulnerabilities of the flesh. Using the literary device of a series of correspondences between a more experienced demon, Uncle Screwtape, and his young apprentice, Wormwood, Lewis brilliantly explores the machinations of evil. In one particularly perceptive letter, Uncle Screwtape tells his nephew, the novice,

> Never forget that when we are dealing with any pleasure in its healthy and normal and satisfying form, we are, in a sense, on the Enemy's ground. I know we have won many a soul through pleasure. All the same, it is His invention, not ours. He made the pleasures: all our research so far has not enabled us to produce one. All we can do is to encourage the humans to take the pleasures which our Enemy has produced, at times, or in ways, or in degrees, which He has forbidden.[18]

Here Lewis astutely depicts the way the devil conspires with our flesh to corrupt God's good intention for his creation. The devil is the great enemy of our souls. His unrelenting cause in the world is the vandalism of shalom.

What Do You Do with Your Chaos?

Not long ago I was having lunch with a friend and lamenting about the chaos that had become my life, droning on about all I was going through. Professional chaos. Relational chaos. Book deadline chaos. On and on I went. When I came to the end of my screed, I expected to receive some expression of empathy or maybe a pat on the back for how well I was doing at keeping it together. But instead I was met with a simple, direct question. "What do you do with all of that?" I didn't quite know what to make of it. The question seemed a bit out of place. But I realized later that it was the sort of thing a spiritual director might ask: "What do you do with your chaos?" He was inviting me to name my strategies for coping with the vandalism of shalom.

When sin enters the biblical story in Genesis 3, the first consequence we see is a profound self-consciousness and an accompanying sense of shame. "Then the eyes of both of them were opened, and they realized they were naked; so they sewed fig leaves together and made coverings for themselves" (Genesis 3:7). In order to deal with their shame, the first couple made clothing out of leaves. I don't know if you've ever seen a fig leaf, but I can assure you this was a profoundly bad idea. But it illustrates the universal tendency of people turned in upon themselves—the tendency to deal with the vandalism of shalom on our own terms, in our own strength, out of our own resources. In our fallen condition we develop deeply ingrained strategies for coping with the vandalism of shalom.

At this moment I have on my desk a handwritten note given to me by a twelve-year-old girl after my sermon last Sunday. It reads,

> My friend, she cut herself. On purpose. I don't know how much pain mentally you must be in to do that. She promised me she would never do it again. But I don't know. She is wearing my bracelet I gave her temporarily. She is such a beautiful girl and fun. I can't comprehend that she did it. I hope she never does it again. And she told me that a ton of other people do it and, ugh. I don't know. She needs help. She's only 12.

Here's the tragic story of a little girl who has developed a strategy for coping with the vandalism of shalom. There's something particularly poignant about it because she's so young and her strategy is so obviously destructive. But it illustrates the reality that is true of all of us.

All of us have become adept at sewing fig leaves. All of us have developed deeply ingrained patterns of responding to the vandalism of shalom, attempting to make life work on our own terms and out of our own resources. It seems to me that there are a handful of common strategies we employ to cope with the vandalism of shalom, when we bump up against the truth that the world is not the way it's supposed to be and we are not the way we are supposed to be.

First, there are strategies of detachment. We don't want to look at the mess that is our world or the brokenness that is our life. Instead we do our best to disengage from the broken places. This often leads us to seek to control the things in our lives that we think we can. We attempt to control people, control things, control circumstances, control our bodies, all in an effort to avoid the reality of chaos, pain and the ache that comes from being a broken person in a broken world. For many people, maintaining the illusion of control is one of the greatest idols of the heart.

Second, there are strategies of distraction. We look away to the "bright, shiny things" of the world to draw our attention away from the reality we don't want to face. Instead of control, we seek to escape, to self-medicate, to numb ourselves to the pain. As Brené Brown has pointed out, "We are the most in debt, obese, addicted, and medicated adult cohort in U. S. history."[19] We reach for cheap shalom substitutes. Shopping. Food. Sex. Alcohol. TV. Noise. Busyness. Productivity. Achievement. Applause. The list could go on and on. We twist good things to make them needed things, becoming dependent on them for their ability to anesthetize us at least for a little while.

Third, there are strategies of despair. We feel completely overwhelmed by the brokenness of our lives and of the world. Despair comes when our sense of control is lost and our attempts at escape leave us empty, so we give up to a sense of helplessness and hopelessness. We lose the capacity to dream of a better future.

Finally, there are strategies of destructiveness. We respond to the reality of the vandalism of shalom by becoming participants in it. We lash out. Sometimes this manifests in overtly self-destructive behavior. Sometimes it is expressed in hostility—violence toward or exploitation of something or someone else. Sometimes it's in tasteful, discreet destructiveness like gossip or lying. Having been bitten, we bite back.

The persistent problem with all of our strategies is that they work. Never fully. Never finally. But enough to keep us coming back to them. This was the problem with Israel's idols in the Old Testament. They prayed to an idol for rain and sometimes it rained. They made oblation to a fertility god and sometimes they conceived. Never mind that the result wasn't because the supposed deities had the power the people thought they did. All the Israelites knew—all they cared about—was that it worked. Our strategies and substitutes can never give us the shalom we long for. But often all we care about is that they work, at least occasionally, at least for a little while. We all move in and out of each of these kinds of strategies and they each manifest themselves in a myriad of different ways. Yet most of us have one default pattern to which we continue to return. We would each do well to name that pattern in our own lives.

Sacred Discontent

Our strategies for coping with the vandalism of shalom have the power they do precisely because they promise to help us with our sense of inadequacy and powerlessness. They promise to help us avoid the suffering that comes with acknowledging the world's brokenness and our brokenness. But as Frederick Buechner has said, "We are never more alive to life than when it hurts—more aware of both our own powerlessness to save ourselves and of at least the possibility of a power beyond ourselves to save us and heal us if we can only open ourselves to it."[20] God's desire is for our sense of powerlessness to drive us to him. The enemies of the soul—the world, the flesh and the devil—want our sense of powerlessness to drive us toward our coping strategies with an even greater urgency and intensity. We unwittingly give in to the plans of these conspirators against shalom when we control, escape, give up or lash out. Each of these strategies only reinforces the incurvature of the soul. They turn us in upon ourselves. God's plan is for our powerlessness to turn us out from ourselves.

There is a response to the reality of the vandalism of shalom that God desires to cultivate in each of us. It is sacred discontent, which I suggested at the beginning of this chapter was the birthplace of missional spirituality. Michael Mangis has said, "God wants to be the God of those who are perpetually discontented. We aren't called to be cynical or negative or distrustful, but God does call us to be discontented."[21] Discontented about what? Discontented that there is still so much brokenness in our lives and in the world. Sacred discontent is that yearning for a better future that comes from being swept up in the dream of God for a world set right that compels us to respond to the vandalism of shalom with indignation and abandon.

Jesus consistently responded to the vandalism of shalom with indignation. He suggested that the kind of life considered blessed by God is the life characterized by mourning over sin and by hungering and thirsting for things to be set right (see Matthew 5:4, 6). The mourning that Jesus talks about in the Beatitudes must begin with acknowledgment of our own complicity in the vandalism of shalom. As Dan Allender has said, "To admit discontent and hunger for redemption requires that we face our part in the problem and compels us to yearn and dream for more."[22]

But our mourning and indignation over the vandalism of shalom cannot be just about us. As Lesslie Newbigin rightly insists, "It is a terrible misunderstanding of the Gospel to think that it offers us salvation while relieving us of responsibility for the life of the world, for the sin and sorrow and pain with which our human life and that of our fellow men and women is so deeply interwoven."[23] We must learn to make the outward turn by seeing, feeling and responding in concrete ways to the reality of brokenness in the world. One of the ways we become people of the outward turn is, not surprisingly, by turning outward. We become people whose lives are characterized by giving ourselves away for the glory of God and the good of other people by, in fact, giving ourselves away for the glory of God and the good of other people. And slowly but persistently over time, we begin to overcome the incurvature of the soul.

But none of this happens out of our own strength. Sacred discontent evokes a response of both indignation and abandon—abandon to a power not our own. Responding to the reality of the vandalism of shalom in our lives and in the world in a way that brings real change requires a power beyond us. It requires abandon to the power of the Spirit, God's empowering presence.

3

The Dwelling Place of God

The Vision of God and the Presence of the Spirit

Spirit of Holiness, you live in the midst of impurity and corruption;
Spirit of Wisdom, you live in the midst of folly; Spirit of truth, you live in one who is
himself deluded. Oh, continue to dwell there, you who do not seek a desirable
dwelling place. . . . Oh, continue to dwell there, that one day you may
finally be pleased by the dwelling which you have prepared in
my heart, foolish, deceiving and impure as it is.

SØREN KIERKEGAARD

The Spirit is given so that we ordinary mortals can become,
in a measure, what Jesus himself was: part of God's future arriving
in the present; a place where heaven and earth meet; the means of God's
kingdom going ahead. The Spirit is given, in fact, so that the church
can share in the life and continuing work of Jesus himself.

N. T. WRIGHT

Life with God for the world is life lived in the presence and power of the
Holy Spirit, the third person of the triune God. But sadly, many Christians today are functional binitarians rather than true trinitarians in

their understanding of and relation to God. God the Father we get (sort of). Jesus the Son we get (perhaps better). But the Holy Spirit? Many of us are not so sure. Some theologians, not without cause, have called the Holy Spirit the "shy member of the Trinity."[1] But perhaps it's appropriate to say he's only shy until you get to know him. New Testament scholar Gordon Fee has called the Holy Spirit "God's empowering presence." He writes, "the Spirit is not merely an impersonal force or influence or power. . . . The Spirit is God's own personal presence in our lives and in our midst."[2] Spirituality—life with God—is life with the Spirit.

Eighteen months ago I found myself wading waist-deep through cold, clear water. The walls of the tunnel surrounding me were barely broader than my shoulders and I had to bend over when the height of the tunnel couldn't accommodate my six-foot frame. Carrying only a tiny LED flashlight, I was leading a group of intrepid travelers through Hezekiah's tunnel, an ancient waterway dug through the mountain on which the city of Jerusalem was built. As its name suggests, the 1,750-foot tunnel was dug during the reign of Israel's king Hezekiah in the eighth century B.C. It allowed water to flow into the ancient city from the Gihon Spring to the Pool of Siloam. The spring still flows and partially fills the tunnel with water to this day. It was an exhilarating experience for me when I emerged from the tunnel and came upon a place that figured prominently in one of my favorite Jesus stories.

The setting of the story was the last day of the Jewish festival of Sukkot, the Feast of Tabernacles. This annual festival celebrated God's provision for his people as they lived in tents in the wilderness for the forty years they wandered there before entering the Promised Land. This last and greatest day of the festival was a day set aside by the ancient Hebrews to plead with God for the provision of water. In the arid climate of the Middle East the people were profoundly conscious of their need for rain from heaven for their survival. On that day the priest would lead a joyous procession from the temple down to the Pool of Siloam—the pool filled by Hezekiah's tunnel—and there he would fill a golden pitcher with the water that had flowed through the ancient tunnel. He would shout out the words of Isaiah 12:3: "With joy you will draw water from the wells of salvation." He would then lead the great procession back up to the temple where he would pour the water out on the altar as a sign of faith, believing that God would supply Israel's great need. It was a symbolic gesture that declared to God, "We're trusting you that there's more to come."

In one ancient Hebrew prayer associated with this last day of the festival, the congregation leader would cry out:

> Our God and the God of our forefathers: Remember the Patriarch [Abraham], who was drawn behind You like water. You blessed him like a tree replanted alongside streams of water. You shielded him, You rescued him from fire and from water. You tested him when he sowed upon all waters.

And the congregation would reply:

> For his sake, do not hold water back!

Then the leader would cry out again:

> Remember the one [Isaac] born with the tidings of, "Let some water be brought." You told his father to slaughter him—to spill his blood like water. He too was scrupulous to pour his heart like water. He dug and discovered wells of water.

And the response would come from the congregation:

> For the sake of his righteousness, grant abundant water![3]

The prayer would continue in this form for several more stanzas, each rehearsing Israel's history down through the ages, showing how prominently water played into the story both literally and figuratively. And after each stanza the people would reply with a request that God "grant abundant water" and "not hold water back."

Somewhere in the midst of all the pomp and circumstance of that day, Jesus stood up and cried out in a loud voice, "Let anyone who is thirsty come to me and drink" (John 7:37). I can only imagine the commotion that undoubtedly accompanied his daring invitation. I love the audacity of Jesus in this story. Earlier in the same chapter, the Gospel writer tells us that the authorities were already after Jesus, trying to kill him. He kept a pretty low profile during the festival until that moment, in the midst of this great day of pleading with God for the provision of water. But in that moment he disrupted the whole affair by claiming that he had the water all thirsty people are longing for.

What Are We Thirsty For?

When Jesus stood up on the last day of the great feast and cried out to the crowd, his audacious invitation—"Let anyone who is thirsty come to me and drink"—contained an implicit question. The question is, "Are you thirsty?" A deep spiritual thirst is a fundamental part of the human condition. We're all thirsty. Jesus' implied question is a rhetorical one. "Do you *realize* you are thirsty?" might be a better way to put it. But if a deep spiritual thirst is characteristic of the human condition, the question for us to ask becomes, "What are we thirsty for?"

We all thirst, whether we know it or not, for the presence of God, the reign of God and the peace of God. In one of the Psalms the ancient poet writes,

As the deer pants for streams of water,
    so my soul pants for you, my God.
My soul thirsts for God, for the living God.
    When can I go and meet with God? (Psalm 42:1-2)

I learned this verse as a kid in a children's song, and I remember always having the image in my mind of a little fawn, Bambi perhaps, scampering through a green meadow surrounded by lush trees and coming upon a flowing stream. When I traveled to Israel for the first time, I came to appreciate the poet's image differently. One doesn't encounter too many green meadows surrounded by lush trees in the Palestinian wilderness. The poet's image is one of desperation. The withered deer is about to die as it stumbles across the parched earth looking for something to satiate its deep thirst. The poet uses that image to speak to our profound yearning to experience the presence of God. "When can I go to meet with God?"

Jesus employs the metaphor of thirst in the Beatitudes when he says, "Blessed are those who hunger and thirst for righteousness, for they will be filled" (Matthew 5:6). Righteousness is a crucial biblical concept, but for many Christians it has become an empty word we use in church that has very little real meaning in our lives. For most of us, it's not something for which we consciously hunger and thirst. If we have any sense of it at all, we usually associate it with moral purity. And it certainly can have connotations of moral uprightness. But the Greek word *dikaiosune* and the Hebrew word *mishpat* can both be translated as "righteousness" or "justice." Perhaps the best way to understand the concept is "set-right-ness." Jesus said, essentially, "Seek first the reign of God and his *dikaiosune*" (Matthew 6:33). The idea he is conveying is not for us to seek first the reign of God and his moral purity. It is to seek first the reign of God and the "set-right-ness" that is the sign and foretaste of its presence. With this understanding in place, we read Jesus' Beatitude again and realize that those he pronounces as blessed are those who hunger and thirst for the "set-right-ness" that characterizes the just reign of God. There's a deep longing in every human heart for things to be set right. Jesus pronounces blessing on those who hunger and thirst for it in ways that cause them to seek after it. He calls on his followers to make the reign of God and his righteousness the priority of their lives.

Finally, the most basic thirst of every person is the thirst for shalom, for the peace that comes about when God's presence and God's reign are fully realized. Saint Augustine famously said, "You have made us for yourself, O Lord, and our hearts are restless until they find their rest in you." The "rest" of which he speaks is the rest of shalom. It is a rest we can experience now in measure but will only experience in fullness when God makes all things new, when earth and heaven are one. Shalom is what we are all made for, so in its absence, we're all desperately thirsty for it.

When Our Thirst Goes Wrong

There's a fascinating little verse about thirst tucked away in the writings of the ancient Hebrew prophet Jeremiah. In Jeremiah 2:13, the Lord, speaking through his prophet, suggests that his people have gone fundamentally wrong by committing two sins. First, the Lord says they have "forsaken me, the spring of living water." God says, in effect, "I am the only one who can meet your deepest needs. I am the only one who can satiate your thirst. And you have forgotten me." Second, the Lord says that his people have not only forgotten him, the fountain of living water, but they have "dug their own cisterns, broken cisterns that cannot hold water." In ancient times people would dig a pit or craft a vessel that would collect and hold rainwater. In employing the metaphor of a broken cistern the prophet is speaking to the human tendency to try to satiate our thirsts out of our own resources, to make life work on our own terms.

The Bible has a word for this recurring human tendency: idolatry. According to John Calvin, our hearts are "perpetual idol-making factories."[4] The sin behind every sin is the breaking of the first commandment, the sin of idolatry. It is the elevation of some thing, some one, some pursuit, some practice to a higher place of loyalty and devotion in our heart than God. In our moments of sin we say to God, "I want this more than I want you. I need this more than I need you. I love this more than I love you." We craft idols. We sew fig leaves. We dig cisterns. We attempt to satiate our thirst out of our own resources. But we're all still thirsty.

Rivers of Living Water

Jesus' audacious invitation "Come to me and drink" was accompanied by a glorious promise: "Whoever believes in me, as Scripture has said, rivers of living water will flow from within them" (John 7:38). The Gospel writer goes on to clarify, saying, "By this he meant the Spirit, whom those who believed in him were later to receive" (John 7:39). According to Jesus, the only solution to our thirst problem is the living water of the Holy Spirit, which is available to all who believe in him. In what sense is this true?

We all thirst for shalom, the dream of God for a world set right. The biblical narrative points us toward a day in which that dream will fully and finally be realized. Everything that is wrong with the world will be made right. Everything that is broken in the world will be made whole. And everything that is marred in the world will be made beautiful. In Ephesians 1:14, the apostle Paul says that the Holy Spirit is given as "a deposit guaranteeing our inheritance." The Greek word translated here as "deposit" is the word *arrabon*. In modern Greek this is the word for an engagement ring, a symbol in the present for that which is coming in the future. N. T. Wright succinctly captures what is the first and perhaps most important thing to grasp about the presence and work of the Holy Spirit: "The Spirit is given to begin the work of making God's future real in the present."[5]

The Spirit has come to bring glimpses and foretastes of the world to come into our world now. Our thirst for shalom is satisfied—not fully or finally, but substantively—as we learn what it means to "walk by the Spirit" (Galatians 5:16). The Bible never promises to take away all our pain or remove us from the brokenness of the world on this side of the new heavens and the new earth. But Jesus does promise rivers of living water to slake our thirst. In order to understand how the Spirit does that, it's helpful to consider what the New Testament has to say about what, precisely, the Spirit has come to do.

What Has the Spirit Come to Do?

First, the Spirit has come to bear witness to the gospel of Jesus. Christian conviction regarding the identity and mission of Jesus is brought about by the persuasive power of the Spirit. In the farewell discourse of John's Gospel, Jesus tells his followers that when the Spirit comes, "he will testify about me" (John 15:26). Elsewhere in the New Testament, the apostle Paul insists that "no one can say, 'Jesus is Lord,' except by the Holy Spirit" (1 Corinthians 12:3). These verses display the New Testament conviction that acquiescence to the truth of Christ and his gospel comes about as a result of the Spirit's work of bearing witness. The witness of the Spirit is not necessarily some palpable work that we can point to and say, "There. I had it." It's not so much something we feel as much as it is something we know in our bones. If we trust Christ in faith, it is because the Spirit has been working his persuasive power in our lives.

In his well-known definition of faith, John Calvin points to this persuasive power of the Holy Spirit. Calvin defines faith as "a firm and certain knowledge of God's benevolence toward us, founded upon the truth of the freely given promise in Christ, both revealed to our minds and sealed upon our hearts through the Holy Spirit."[6] During my days as a doctoral student, I spent quite a bit of time studying this definition from Calvin and its theological implications (sounds exciting, I know). But the longer I sat with it the more I found myself troubled by it. Not troubled theologically. Troubled existentially. Calvin defines faith as a "firm and certain knowledge." When I examine my own faith, "firm" and "certain" are not often adjectives that I would use to describe it. There have been long seasons of my life where "thin" and "fragile" were much more appropriate. I have struggled deeply with doubt.

Thankfully I didn't give up reading Calvin, and later I discovered that Calvin the pastor nuances Calvin the theologian. He writes, "Surely, while we teach that faith ought to be certain and assured, we cannot imagine any certainty that is not tinged with doubt, or any assurance that is not assailed by some anxiety. On the other hand, we say that believers are in perpetual conflict with their own unbelief."[7] Those sentences were life-giving to me. I know what it is to live in "perpetual conflict" with my own unbelief. So what Calvin has in view when he talks about faith being firm and certain is not so much a quality of faith as it is a kind of tenacity of faith. Calvin goes on to say, "Far, indeed, are we from putting their consciences in any peaceful repose, undisturbed by any tumult at all. Yet, once again, we deny that, in whatever way they are afflicted, they fall away and depart from the certain assurance received from God's mercy."[8] Christian faith is not above tumult and affliction, but it holds tenaciously to the promise of mercy. And the tenacity of that faith is not a human achievement. It is the Spirit's inner work of persuasion that helps us to continue believing that God is kindly disposed toward us because of the work of Jesus on our behalf.

Second, the Spirit has come to bring us the life of Jesus. In John's Gospel, Jesus talks a lot about life, and a particular kind of life at that. He speaks repeatedly of *zoe aionion*. This little phrase is often translated in our English Bibles as "eternal life." The downside of this translation is that it seems to emphasize—at least in the minds of many— the duration of the life Jesus came to bring rather than the kind of life Jesus came to bring. Also, it tends to be regarded as the life we will enter into in the future, after our death. But the phrase as Jesus used it was about bringing the life of the future into the present. Judaism taught that eternal life would appear only in God's last day, or in the age to come. John tells the Jesus story in a way that shows that this eschatological day of salvation has already arrived in the person of Jesus. Eternity has broken into history. In Jesus, the life of the age to come breaks into the present age. And this life is not simply about there and then but about here and now. "Very truly I tell you, the one who believes has the life of the age to come" (John 6:47, my translation). The hope of the resurrection and the renewal of all things is

indeed a glorious hope, but Jesus brought with him the life of that
world into this one.

And that life comes to us by the work of the Spirit. "The Spirit gives life,"
Jesus said (John 6:63). In the same vein, the apostle Paul writes, "Therefore,
there is now no condemnation for those who are in Christ Jesus, because
through Christ Jesus the law of the Spirit who gives life has set you free
from the law of sin and death" (Romans 8:1-2). The ancient creed of the
church declares, "We believe in the Holy Spirit, the Lord, the giver of life."
The Spirit brings us the life of Jesus, the life of the age to come.

Third, the Spirit has come to conform us to the image of Jesus. The
apostle Paul wrote to the Christians in Galatia, "I am again in the pains
of childbirth until Christ is formed in you" (Galatians 4:19). Paul seized
upon a powerful metaphor to capture his passion for the spiritual
formation of these Galatian believers. His intense passion—likened
to labor pains—was to see Christ formed in them, to see the character of Jesus deeply impressed on their hearts and beautifully dis-
played in their lives. Elsewhere Paul says this is the destiny of every
Christian: "For those God foreknew he also predestined to be conformed to the image of his Son, that he might be the firstborn among
many brothers and sisters" (Romans 8:29). Interestingly, this statement
comes immediately on the heels of a New Testament promise that is
a favorite to many Christians: "And we know that in all things God
works for the good of those who love him, who have been called
according to his purpose" (Romans 8:28). This immediate context
would seem to indicate that the good God is working all things toward
is his purpose of transforming us to the image of Jesus. God employs
even our suffering in this grand intention for our lives. This transformation is not merely an external conformity to a set of behavioral
standards. But neither is it a merely internal work on the heart. To
become like Jesus is to be transformed from the inside out, from the
deepest desires and affections of the heart to the patterns of relating
with others in the world.

According to Paul, this kind of transformation can't be self-generated. It is the work of the Spirit in us that makes us like Jesus. In 2 Corinthians Paul writes, "And we all, who with unveiled faces contemplate the Lord's glory, are being transformed into his image with ever-increasing glory, which comes from the Lord, who is the Spirit" (2 Corinthians 3:18). It is the destiny of every Christian to be transformed into the image of Jesus, and this, Paul says, is what the Spirit is up to in each of our lives.

It's important that we understand that becoming like Jesus does not merely mean becoming holy, in the narrow ways that term is often understood. It isn't just a matter of moral purity, of being unsoiled by the world. Becoming like Jesus means learning increasingly to imitate his incarnate life. If we are to become like Jesus we need a clear vision of what he was like. That will be the focus of the next chapter. But for now it can suffice to say that Jesus was the incarnate one who dwelt among us to accomplish the mission of God. If we want to become like him, then we too must learn what it means to live a missional life by the power of the Spirit in the places we dwell.

This recognition leads us to say, finally, that the Spirit has come to empower us for the mission of Jesus. In the first chapter of the book of Acts, as Luke picks up the story of Jesus after his resurrection, he writes,

> After his suffering, he presented himself to them and gave many convincing proofs that he was alive. He appeared to them over a period of forty days and spoke about the kingdom of God. On one occasion, while he was eating with them, he gave them this command: "Do not leave Jerusalem, but wait for the gift my Father promised, which you have heard me speak about. For John baptized with water, but in a few days you will be baptized with the Holy Spirit."
>
> Then they gathered around him and asked him, "Lord, are you at this time going to restore the kingdom to Israel?"

He said to them: "It is not for you to know the times or dates the Father has set by his own authority. But you will receive power when the Holy Spirit comes on you; and you will be my witnesses in Jerusalem, and in all Judea and Samaria, and to the ends of the earth." (Acts 1:3-8)

Luke's words show us that the priority of Jesus' teaching after his resurrection was still the inbreaking of the reign of God. The question that the disciples ask, concerning the restoration of the kingdom to Israel, demonstrates that they still had a more narrow understanding of the reign of God than Jesus did. The kingdom vision of Jesus was cosmic in scope. He called them to bear witness to the ends of the earth.

Jesus' words make clear that the task entrusted to his followers would require a power beyond them. They needed the power of the Spirit. It's important to note that when the Spirit's power is highlighted in the teaching of Jesus, it's not for the personal benefit of the "insiders." The power of the Spirit is not principally about the ecstatic spiritual experience of the Spirit-filled follower of Jesus but about the empowerment of that follower to participate in the mission of God. N. T. Wright has said it well:

> Despite what you might think from some excitement in the previous generation about new spiritual experiences, God doesn't give people the Holy Spirit in order to let them enjoy the spiritual equivalent of a day at Disneyland. Of course, if you're downcast and gloomy, the fresh wind of God's Spirit can and often does give you a new perspective on everything, and above all grants a sense of God's presence, love, comfort, and even joy. But the point of the Spirit is to enable those who follow Jesus to take into all the world the news that he is Lord, that he has won the victory over the forces of evil, that a new world has opened up, and that we are to help make it happen.[9]

The Spirit has come to empower God's people to engage the mission of Jesus.

In his book *The Road to Missional*, Michael Frost—drawing on the seminal work of the South African missiologist David Bosch—suggests that the essence of the mission of Jesus' disciples, then and now, is alerting people to the reign of God through Christ.[10] This work of alerting people to the universal reign of God through Christ involves both our announcement and our demonstration of that reign. Frost writes,

> If mission is the alerting of people to the reign of God through Christ, our mandate is to do whatever is required in the circumstances to both demonstrate and announce that kingship. We feed the hungry because in the world to come there will be no such thing as starvation. We share Christ because in the world to come there will be no such thing as unbelief. Both are the fashioning of foretastes of that world to come, none more or less valid or important than the other.[11]

The Spirit has come to bring us foretastes of the world to come—to begin the work of making God's future real in the present—and to empower us to dream up and fashion foretastes of the world to come in the ways we announce and demonstrate the universal reign of God through Christ.

The Dwelling Place of God

I'm convinced we need a new translation of the Bible, the TNIV: the Texas New International Version. That's because in standard English there is no distinction between singular and plural when it comes to the form of the second person pronoun. I can say "you" and refer to a single person or to a group of people. But in Greek, the language of the original writings of the New Testament, the distinction is clear. They are two completely different words. No reader of the original language would ever confuse whether the author was referring to an individual or to a community. But in English, where our penchant for individualism is ever-present, the ambiguity is almost inescapable. That's where the vernacular of my home state comes in. In Texas, we have a perfectly legitimate way of distinguishing between the second person singular and the second person plural. There's "you." And there's "y'all."

I'm convinced that it would transform the way American Christians read their Bibles if every time they came across the word *you* and thought it was about "me," they would see the word *y'all* and realize that it's about "us." The spirituality on display throughout the Bible is never simply about "me and my God" but always about "us and our God."

Here are just a few examples of what the "Texas NIV" would look like:

Y'all are the salt of the earth. . . . Y'all are the light of the world. (Matthew 5:13, 14)

Christ in y'all, the hope of glory. (Colossians 1:27)

It is God who works in y'all to will and to act in order to fulfill his good purpose. (Philippians 2:13)

But perhaps my favorite example, and maybe the one with the most theological freight, is 1 Corinthians 3:16. Here's how it would read in the Texas version:

Don't y'all know that y'all are God's temple and that God's Spirit dwells in y'all? If anyone destroys God's temple, God will destroy that person; for God's temple is sacred, and y'all are that temple.

It would be easy for an English-speaking reader to see the word "you" in a standard translation of this text and assume that it was a statement about individual believers. But Paul is making a radical, communal claim here. Throughout the biblical narrative, the temple was more than a place of worship. The temple was the place where heaven and earth intersected. The temple was the dwelling place of God. Here Paul makes a radical claim about the temple, the dwelling place of God. The dwelling place of God is the church. "Y'all are God's temple." Despite all the ways we get things wrong and mess things up, we are the temple of God and the Holy Spirit dwells in our midst.

In an essay on early Christian community, Orthodox theologian John Zizioulas writes,

> Christian spirituality could not be experienced outside the community. . . . Individualism is incompatible with Christian spirituality. None can possess the Spirit as an individual, but only as a member of the community. When the Spirit blows the result is never to create good individual Christians but members of a community.[12]

When Zizioulas suggests that "none can possess the Spirit as an individual," he's not saying we are incapable of experiencing the Spirit personally but that we don't experience the Spirit privately, in a life of isolation from the life of the church. Christian spirituality—life with the Spirit—is life lived in and with the community of faith. The dominant question in American Christianity has tended to be, "Do you have a personal relationship with Jesus?" But perhaps we need to ask, "Do you have a communal relationship with Jesus?" My personal relationship with Jesus is formed, shaped and sustained in and by my communal relationship with Jesus. Christian spirituality is "the whole person's participation and formation in the church—Christ's body, the Spirit's public—which exists to entice and call the world back to its Creator, its true purpose, and its only real hope."[13]

The church is the temple of God, the dwelling place of the Spirit. It's crucial that we understand "church" in this discussion not as "a place where" but as "a people who." The church is the community of faith. The Spirit is not confined to a building but is present and active among a people. In his work in and through the church, the Spirit bears witness to the gospel of Jesus, brings us the life of Jesus, conforms us to the image of Jesus and empowers us for the mission of Jesus. As each of these statements implies, the work of the Spirit is not about drawing attention to himself but is rather about turning our attention to Jesus. As J. I. Packer has said, "The Spirit's message is never, 'Look at me; listen to me; come to me; get to know me,' but always 'Look at *him*, and see his glory; listen to *him*, and hear his word; go to *him*, and have life."[14] In light of this reality, we would do well to give more sustained attention to the embodied life of Jesus, the pattern into which the Spirit is molding us.

Glimpses of the World to Come

The Vision of God and the Way of Jesus

*Christ came into the world with the purpose of saving the world,
but also with the purpose—this in turn is implicit in his first purpose—
of being the prototype, of leaving footprints for the person who
wanted to join him, who then might become an imitator.*

SØREN KIERKEGAARD

*Let it then be our main concern
to meditate on the life of Jesus Christ.*

THOMAS À KEMPIS

Jesus never talked about "spirituality" per se. That's our word, not his. But reflecting on spirituality in the way of Jesus helps us in the overarching concern of this book—the recovery of a spirituality deeply informed by the logic of the incarnation—by reminding us that the incarnation is not simply a principle that shapes the way we think about spirituality. It refers us to the historical, embodied life— the way of Jesus—that provides a model we are called to pattern our lives after.

The historic creeds of the church have always insisted that Jesus was both fully God and fully human. In the great mystery of our faith, the church confesses that this one who was "true God from true God" also "came down from heaven" and "was made man." Against challenges to the nascent orthodoxy coming from both directions, the early church insisted that he was not the divine one who only appeared to be human nor the human one merely endued with divine power; he was and is "perfect in Godhead and also perfect in manhood, truly God and truly man."

The insistence that Jesus was fully human is most strongly associated in the tradition with the understanding that we humans needed a human mediator. Only as a human could he atone for the sins of humanity. Only as a resurrected human could he secure the promise of resurrection for humanity. But the church's insistence that Jesus was fully human also has profound implications for Christian spirituality. As fully God, Jesus shows us in his life what God is like. But as fully human, he shows us what humanity is intended to be. As Kierkegaard has said, he came to be the "prototype" of a new humanity.[1] Jesus' life shows us what it looks like to live out our human vocation in the midst of this broken world while we wait for the dream of God to come true in all its fullness.

But this insistence points us to another reason it's helpful to talk about spirituality in the way of Jesus. As we've said from the beginning, to speak of a distinctly Christian spirituality is not primarily to speak of the "interior life"—the human spirit—but to speak of the totality of life lived in the power of the Holy Spirit. To speak of Christian spirituality is to speak of the third person of the Trinity present and active in the whole of human life. Thus, spirituality in the way of Jesus is about living the kind of life Jesus modeled by the enabling power of the Spirit at work in us. As I argued in the previous chapter, this is precisely the point of the Spirit's present work in the world.

So spirituality in the way of Jesus is no mere human achievement.

The call to live like Jesus, to pattern our lives after his, cannot be heard as a simple call to moralism or activism. It cannot be construed as something one can accomplish by trying harder. It is fundamentally misunderstood if taken to refer to an ethical example accompanied by an admonition to "go and do likewise." It must be understood, instead, as a call to live in openness to and dependence on the Spirit in a way that enables us to live into the story of Jesus, to imitate him, in the concrete realities of our lives. While the pursuit of Jesus as an ethical example may be a noble intention, the full meaning of "the imitation of Christ" is impossible to attain apart from the transforming and empowering presence of the Spirit.

In order to live out the kind of life Jesus modeled by the enabling power of the Spirit, we need to look more closely at that way of life. As I've studied the Gospels, I have identified four aspects of his character that capture the kind of life he has called his followers to imitate. Jesus was a boundary breaker, a shalom maker, a people keeper and a wounded healer.

Jesus the Boundary Breaker

In 1912 the Princeton theologian B. B. Warfield published an essay called "The Emotional Life of Our Lord" in which he undertook a study of the Gospels to discover what words the Gospel writers used to describe the emotional dispositions of Jesus. The word that Warfield discovered was used more often than any other to describe Jesus' emotional life was *compassion*. Frederick Buechner helpfully defines compassion as "that fatal capacity for feeling what it is like to live inside somebody else's skin. It is the knowledge that there can never really be any peace and joy for me until there is peace and joy finally for you too."[2]

Jesus' compassion was one of the most powerful shaping factors in his life. And it led him to disregard and decry the powerful but artificial boundaries contrived by people. Because of his great compassion,

Jesus touched the untouchable, loved the unlovable and forgave the unforgivable. Jesus lived in a society full of boundaries: boundaries between Jews and Gentiles, between clean and unclean, between the righteous and sinners, between rich and poor, between men and women. Yet Jesus persistently and subversively traversed all of those culturally imposed boundaries.

There is something remarkable about the reputation Jesus developed. By his own admission, he was considered "a glutton and a drunkard, a friend of tax collectors and sinners" (Luke 7:34; Matthew 11:19). It's worth asking whether anything remotely close to that could ever be said about us or about the faith communities of which we are a part. And if not, what does that say about the degree to which we actually look like Jesus?

My suggestion here is not that we actually become gluttons and drunkards, but merely to observe that this depiction of Jesus' character seems to make it clear that he knew how to throw a good dinner party. Jesus threw the kind of dinner parties that no one wanted to miss except the uptight religious people of his day who didn't like the guest list. Table fellowship with Jesus was an inclusive act of compassion and hospitality with profound theological significance. According to New Testament scholar James D. G. Dunn, "In the Middle East the table had a quasi-sacred character. It was a religious act: It expressed religious obligations and was reinforced by religious sanctions. This made the sharing of a meal, the act of hospitality, something sacred in turn."[3] The breaking and sharing of bread was a sacred act of acceptance and friendship.

We can hardly appreciate the scandal Jesus created by sharing a table with tax collectors and sinners. In first-century Israel, tax collectors were among the most despised members of society because they made their living as agents of the Roman occupation, enforcing the exploitative Roman policies for their own financial gain. Their work was seen as collaboration with the enemy. They were joined at

Jesus' table by "sinners" who were despised by the pious members of the community as violators of the divine law. These were the "notorious sinners" whose offenses against God were not merely private indiscretions but a matter of public knowledge. They were the objects of scorn and to be avoided at all costs—they were considered not just notorious but contagious. Contact with them was a blemish on one's own moral rectitude and standing in the society.

The scandal created by Jesus' close association with these despised ones was not, however, merely a reaction to his questionable choice of friends. It came about because that act of boundary breaking was directly related to Jesus' announcement of the inbreaking of the kingdom of God. According to N. T. Wright:

> The objection did not arise because Jesus was teaching or propagating a different religious system; nor because he was letting wicked people carry on with their sin and pretending all was well; nor because Jesus, as a private individual, was associating with people who were "beyond the pale." There was no reason to suppose the Pharisees, or anyone else, spied on ordinary people who were "associating" with "sinners" and angrily objected to them doing so. Accusations were leveled, rather, because this welcome to sinners was being offered *precisely by someone announcing the kingdom of god*, and, moreover, offering this welcome as itself a vital part of that kingdom.[4]

According to Jesus, the reign of God that he came to bring was not just for the insiders, the pious ones who lived upright lives. It was for the outsiders, those on the margins: the poor, the weak, the broken, the "notorious sinners."

When Jesus looked at people who were far from God he did not view them with scorn and derision. He saw them with compassion because they were "harassed and helpless, like sheep without a shepherd" (Matthew 9:36). Jesus' compassion moved him to cross culturally imposed boundaries and to pursue friendship and solidarity with those who were on the margins of their society. When challenged over his table fellowship with tax collectors and sinners—crossing what the Pharisees believed to be divinely sanctioned boundaries— Jesus insisted, "It is not the healthy who need a doctor, but the sick. I have not come to call the righteous, but sinners" (Mark 2:17).

To pursue spirituality in the way of Jesus is to become a boundary breaker. Like Jesus, we live in a world full of a wide variety of culturally imposed boundaries: boundaries of race and ethnicity, of socio-economic status, of political loyalties, and of religion and lifestyle. We have our own conceptions of notorious sinners. We have people who live on the margins of our society. Yet we find it all too easy to live out a comfortable Christian existence entirely within the boundaries our culture has created.

My friend Heather is a boundary breaker. Heather's husband is a successful professional athlete. They live in a beautiful home in one of the most affluent neighborhoods in our community. They could easily sit back and enjoy the fruit of their success, walled off from the rest of the world and its brokenness. Heather could live comfortably within the boundaries her economic status provides. But Heather is a fol-lower of Jesus and has experienced the transforming work of the Spirit. Heather understands that Jesus was a boundary breaker and that he longs for her to be one too.

So Heather has begun to invest herself heavily in the local women's jail. She goes regularly to one unit where she has begun to build friend-ships with women who are at the opposite end of the economic spectrum. She mentors these women, focusing on life skills that will help them after their release. And she teaches them the Bible and the love, acceptance and forgiveness they can experience through Jesus. She shares meals and life with our society's notorious sinners. Heather knows that in the world to come there will not be the need for jail cells that keep some people in and other people out. She knows that the boundaries that now distinguish her from the women in those jail cells will be made obsolete. So she's chosen to imitate the compassion of Jesus and cross those boundaries now.

②Jesus the Shalom Maker

Everywhere Jesus went, glimpses of shalom showed up. As Gabriel Fackre puts it, "The Incarnation of the Vision of Shalom manifests itself in miracles of shalom."[5] The Gospel writers indicate that the two most characteristic features of Jesus' ministry were his proclamation of the "gospel [*euangelion*] of the kingdom" and his mighty deeds of exorcism and healing. And in their depiction, these two went hand in hand. Jesus never used his miraculous power for public relations purposes. He didn't do miracles as a marketing strategy to attract more listeners to hear his message. Rather, the miracles were directly tied to the gospel he was proclaiming. He proclaimed the gospel and brought glimpses of shalom.

In the Septuagint, the Greek translation of the Old Testament, you find that the word for "gospel" occurs most frequently as a verb *euangelizo*, which simply means, "to proclaim good news." The greatest concentration of occurrences of the word comes in the book of Isaiah in the context of the expectation of a coming agent of God who will bring liberation and renewal to exiled Israel. One such occurrence in Isaiah 52:7 provides crucial insight:

> How beautiful on the mountains
>   are the feet of those who bring good news,
> who proclaim peace,
>   who bring good tidings,
>   who proclaim salvation,
> who say to Zion, "Your God reigns!"

Here we have Isaiah's poetic depiction of what it means to speak of "good news." While in English we are accustomed to poetry that repeats rhyme or meter, Hebrew uses the repetition of ideas, drawing poetic parallels between one line and the next. Thus in this passage there is an essential connection between good news, peace, salvation and the reign of God.

The gospel Jesus came to proclaim and embody was the gospel of shalom, the gospel of salvation, the gospel of the reign of God. And Jesus claimed that in his ministry the reign of God was breaking into the world. His miracles were demonstrations of the inbreaking of the reign of God. Where Jesus encountered the vandalism of shalom, he brought glimpses of the world to come.

In his book *God the Peacemaker*, Graham Cole argues that even the work of Jesus on the cross must be understood in terms of his pursuit of this robust biblical vision of peace. The subtitle of Cole's book is *How Atonement Brings Shalom*. He writes, "There is no shalom . . . without sacrifice. Peace is made through the blood of the cross. The atoning life, death and vindication of the faithful Son bring shalom by addressing the problem of sin, death, the devil and wrath definitely."[6] It is because of Jesus' sacrifice, satisfaction, substitution and victory that the triune God's reconciling project will one day finally see "God's people in God's place under God's rule living God's way enjoying shalom in God's holy and loving presence to God's glory."[7]

All of this brings us back to Jesus' statement in the Beatitudes: "Blessed are the shalom makers, for they will be called sons of God." Jesus is not saying that people earn the privilege of being God's children by being shalom makers. Rather, he is using a culturally recognized idiom to refer to a person's character. To be called a "son of" something or someone was a way of saying that your character bears a resemblance to that thing or that person. For example, the disciples James and John are given the nickname "sons of thunder." In the book of Acts, Barnabas is given his name because it means "son of encouragement." (We occasionally speak to a person's character by using a crass "son of a . . ." idiom today, but that's another story.)

When Jesus says, "Blessed are the shalom makers, for they will be called sons of God," he is saying that to be a person who invests his or her life in the pursuit of shalom is to be like God, to resemble his character, to be about his work in the world. To pursue spirituality in the way of Jesus is to become a shalom maker the way Jesus was a shalom maker. To be conformed—inside and out—to the character of Christ means that we invest ourselves in the pursuit of wholeness, harmony, flourishing and delight for God's image bearers and God's creation. As Nicholas Wolterstorff has said:

> Shalom is both God's cause in the world and our human calling. Even though the full incursion of shalom into our history will be divine gift and not merely human achievement, even though its episodic incursion into our lives now also has a dimension of divine gift, nonetheless it is shalom that we are to work and struggle for. We are not to stand around, hands folded, waiting for shalom to arrive. We are workers in God's cause, his peace-workers.[8]

Where we encounter the vandalism of shalom, our calling is to be like Jesus, bringing with us glimpses of the world to come. It is not too much to say that the credibility of our proclamation of the gospel is intimately tied to the ways in which we demonstrate the inbreaking of the reign of God in our lives and in the world.

My friend Rob is a shalom maker. He is the cofounder of an organization called Love146. In 2002 Rob traveled with a small group of friends to Southeast Asia. While there, they went with a group of undercover investigators into one of the many brothels that participate in the trafficking and commercial sexual exploitation of children. The statistics regarding this horrific crime are staggering. It is estimated that two children are bought and sold around the world every minute. But for Rob to see this grim reality up close was almost unbearable. He found himself standing in a room looking through glass windows at little girls wearing red dresses. Each girl had a number pinned to her dress that allowed customers to identify which one they wanted. The girls sat watching cartoons, staring into the television sets with lifeless expressions. But there was one little girl who wasn't staring robotically at the TV screens, one little girl who still had fight left in her eyes. She was staring defiantly through the glass toward the men on the other side. Her number was 146.

Rob and his friends founded Love146 in her honor. According to its website, love146.org, the organization "works toward the abolition of child trafficking and exploitation through prevention and aftercare solutions while contributing to a growing abolition movement." Rob and his team are doing incredible work both internationally and domestically to combat one of the most heinous crimes in the world today.

Rob could easily have chosen to ignore the reality of child sex slavery when confronted with it. He didn't have to be in that brothel on that night. But Rob is a follower of Jesus who has experienced the transforming work of the Spirit. Rob understands that Jesus was a shalom maker and that he longs for him to be one too. Rob knows that in the world to come there will be no children exploited, no injustice tolerated, no lives wrecked by greed and perversion. Rob shares in the dream of God and therefore has chosen to leverage his life for the cause of shalom.

Jesus the People Keeper

The Gospel of Mark is the shortest, most compact account of the four Gospels. When Mark tells the story of Jesus, things move quickly. So it's interesting to note how early in the story Mark indicates that Jesus has raised the ire of religious leaders to such a degree that they begin to plot how they might kill him. On Mark's account it occurs early in the third chapter, on the heels of two controversies surrounding the Sabbath. In the first scene Jesus and his disciples are walking through a field on the Sabbath and decide to pick some of the heads of grain for food. The Pharisees become indignant at what they take to be a violation of the law. In the second scene Jesus heals a man with a shriveled hand on the Sabbath day in the synagogue. Once again the Pharisees feel that what Jesus did is an affront to God's law of the Sabbath. After this second occurrence Mark says the Pharisees have begun to conspire to kill him (Mark 3:6).

It's difficult for contemporary readers to understand just how seriously the Jews of Jesus' day took the Sabbath. The command to honor the Sabbath day and keep it holy was one of the Ten Commandments, the very foundation of the ethical life of the people of God. The theology of the Sabbath was rooted in creation and the exodus. It was one of the primary markers of participation in the covenant community of Israel.

But as both controversies make clear, Jesus refused to do what the Pharisees had done, which was to elevate the status of the Sabbath to a higher place of importance than people who were made in God's image. Jesus said to the Pharisees, "The Sabbath was made for man, not man for the Sabbath" (Mark 2:27). Without denying the significance of Sabbath, Jesus insisted that human beings are of infinitely greater value. The Sabbath was made for them and not the other way around. According to Jesus, what ultimately matters to God is not Sabbath keeping but people keeping.[9]

Where did Jesus get the idea that what ultimately matters to God is not so much observance of religious rules and rituals but caring for people in need? I believe he found that to be the clear implication of the teaching of the Hebrew prophets. In one of the most striking examples of this in the Old Testament, the Lord speaks through the prophet Isaiah in Isaiah 1:11-15, saying,

"The multitude of your sacrifices—
    what are they to me?" says the LORD.
"I have more than enough of burnt offerings,
    of rams and the fat of fattened animals;

I have no pleasure
    in the blood of bulls and lambs and goats.
When you come to appear before me,
    who has asked this of you,
    this trampling of my courts?
Stop bringing meaningless offerings!
    Your incense is detestable to me.
New Moons, Sabbaths and convocations—
    I cannot bear your worthless assemblies.
Your New Moon feasts and your appointed festivals
    I hate with all my being.
They have become a burden to me;
    I am weary of bearing them.
When you spread out your hands in prayer,
    I hide my eyes from you;
even when you offer many prayers,
    I am not listening."

What is so remarkable in this passage is that the practices described as utterly detestable to God are things he has commanded of his people. The prophet lists those rituals and ceremonies that marked Israel as the covenant community of God. Yet he says they are meaningless and worthless. Why? The prophet continues in Isaiah 1:15-17:

Your hands are full of blood!
Wash and make yourselves clean.
    Take your evil deeds out of my sight;
    stop doing wrong.
Learn to do right; seek justice.
    Defend the oppressed.
Take up the cause of the fatherless;
    plead the case of the widow.

The prophet makes it clear that God looks disdainfully at the "spiritual disciplines" of his people because they had been complicit in or tolerated injustice and exploitation. Their acts of piety were meaningless if they did not care for the broken and abused among God's image bearers.

Spirituality in the way of Jesus is not primarily about rule keeping or ritual keeping. It's about people keeping. To be sure, there are life-giving formative practices that are a vital part of Christian spirituality. These practices will be discussed at length in the pages that follow. But the practices are not the point. The point is caring for what God cares about—namely, bringing hope, healing, reconciliation, equality, justice and mercy to people created in his image.

My friend Leette is a people keeper. She works as a nurse on the seventh floor of a hospital just a few blocks from my office in downtown Dallas. I first met Leette when she was taking care of my sister. At first I would see Leette only when I happened to come for a visit when Leette was on duty. But before long I began seeing Leette much more. The seventh floor of Roberts Hospital is the cancer ward, and my sister was in the final stages of a battle with kidney cancer. During the last few weeks of her life I practically moved in to the hospital to be her primary caretaker. It was then that I began to see how Leette went beyond her professional obligations in caring for her patients. The tenderness, compassion and attentive concern she demonstrated in those difficult days offered a profound sense of comfort and strength to my family as we tried to bear up under that painful burden.

One evening during one of the most physically and emotionally difficult periods of the entire ordeal, I pulled Leette aside to tell her what I saw as I watched her work. I told her that my faith told me a day was coming when there wouldn't be a seventh floor of Roberts Hospital, when there wouldn't be a cancer ward, when there wouldn't be debilitating disease and when the people we loved would no longer die. And I told her that as I watched her work among the people who suffered under the weight of the world as it is right now, I saw her bring glimpses of the world that's coming.

Leette could have chosen from a host of other vocations in life. And even as a nurse she could have served in any number of other less difficult places. She didn't have to be on that cancer ward during the last few weeks of my sister's life. But Leette is a follower of Jesus and has experienced the transforming work of the Spirit. Leette understands that Jesus was a people keeper and that he longs for her to be one too. Leette knows that a day is coming when there will be no more death or mourning or crying or pain. But she also knows that day hasn't arrived yet. So Leette has chosen to invest her life now in easing the burden of people who are suffering under the weight of the world that's not yet been made new.

Jesus the Wounded Healer

There can be no more profound an example of the way that Jesus was a boundary breaker, shalom maker or people keeper than the example of the cross. The cross of Christ is an act of divine compassion that makes possible the offer of divine hospitality, the welcome of God at the banquet table of the kingdom. The cross is the means by which the dream of God, the dream of shalom, is made secure, as Jesus willingly submits himself to all of the injustice and cruelty that sin and death have to offer and triumphs over them, trampling death by death. And all of this is undertaken to rescue, reconcile and renew God's broken, rebellious image bearers. "God wants shalom and will pay any price to get it back. Human sin is stubborn, but not as stubborn as the grace of God and not half so persistent, not half so ready to suffer to win its way."[10]

In the cross we find one final aspect of the life of Jesus that we are called to imitate. Jesus was a wounded healer. In the poetic depiction of the suffering servant, written centuries before Jesus' life but in prophetic anticipation of all that he would accomplish, Isaiah writes,

> Surely he took up our pain
> > and bore our suffering,
> yet we considered him punished by God,
> > stricken by him, and afflicted.
> But he was pierced for our transgressions,
> > he was crushed for our iniquities;
> the punishment that brought us peace [shalom] was on him,
> > and by his wounds we are healed. (Isaiah 53:4-5)

Jesus suffered vicariously on behalf of all humanity to bring us shalom. By his wounds we are healed. He has made his wounds available to us as the means of our healing and salvation.

I first read Henri Nouwen's classic little book *The Wounded Healer* in 1999 when I was sitting at my father's bedside during the last days of his life. In the midst of that experience, when I felt like my heart had an open wound, God used Nouwen's words like a salve. That experience has marked me deeply and given me invaluable perspective and empathy as a husband, father, pastor and friend. The essence of Nouwen's book is captured in his own words when he writes,

> Nobody escapes being wounded. We all are wounded people, whether physically, emotionally, mentally, or spiritually. The main question is not, "How can we hide our wounds?" so we don't have to be embarrassed, but "How can we put our woundedness in the service of others?" When our wounds cease to be a source of shame, and become a source of healing, we have become wounded healers.

Jesus was God's wounded healer: through his wounds we are healed. Jesus' suffering and death brought joy and life. His humiliation brought glory; his rejection brought a community of love. As followers of Jesus we can also allow our wounds to bring healing to others.[11]

The apostle Paul tells us that "the God and Father of our Lord Jesus Christ" is "the Father of compassion and the God of all comfort, who comforts us in all our troubles, so that we can comfort those in trouble with the comfort we ourselves receive from God" (2 Corinthians 1:3-4). All of us have experienced the vandalism of shalom through our own foolish, sinful choices, through what others have done to us, or through merely living in the midst of a fallen world. But in Christ, through his wounds, we find comfort and healing. Spirituality in the way of Jesus is about learning to be used as instruments of his healing grace in the lives of others as we make our wounds available to them.

My friend Lauri is a wounded healer. Lauri ran away from home when she was fourteen. As happens all too often with runaway girls, Lauri was discovered in her vulnerable state and violated by people who acted as though they wanted to help her. She was raped by four men. From that time, Lauri believed that she was "damaged goods," dirty and worthless. Before long she found herself addicted to drugs and alcohol and making her living in the sex industry.

After years of being exploited, Lauri found help. She found a way out and eventually she found Jesus. Through the loving care of a faithful community of Christians who embodied the grace of God in her life, Lauri received care and nurture in her faith. She entered counseling and recovery and experienced healing and freedom from her shame and addictions. Now Lauri works as an advocate and mentor for women who are trying to leave the sex industry. She helps them find new skills, new jobs, new places to live and new ways of life. She's able to connect and empathize with them in ways few others can. She's able to combat the lies many of them have come to believe about themselves and to teach them the truth of Christ and his mercy. She's able to make her own wounds available to them as a source of healing in their lives.

Lauri could have stayed away from the pain of her past. She didn't have to reenter that world to help rescue women from it. But Lauri is a follower of Jesus and has experienced the transforming power of the Spirit. Lauri understands that Jesus is a wounded healer and that he longs for her to be one too. Laurie knows that in the world that is to come there will not be any more exploitation. She knows that the wounds of our pasts will be fully and finally healed. And so Lauri has chosen to make her wounds available to others, to be used by Jesus as an instrument of his healing grace.

Conclusion

Jesus Christ came into the world to save the world—to secure, by his death and resurrection, the dream of God, the dream of shalom. But he also came into the world to be the prototype of a new humanity, to show us what it means to live out our human vocation in this broken world as we wait for the dream of God to come in its fullness. For us to live out a spirituality deeply informed by the logic of the incarnation—life with God for the world—is for us to pattern our lives after the life of Jesus who was a boundary breaker, a shalom maker, a people keeper, and a wounded healer. In order to pursue this repatterning of our lives, God has given us a set of embodied practices—the spiritual disciplines—through which the Spirit does his work of making us more like Jesus.

5

A Grammar of the Disciplines

Practicing the Vision in Everyday Life

When we carry out our "religious duties" we are like people
digging channels in a waterless land, in order that when
at last the water comes, it may find them ready.

C. S. LEWIS

Ascetic practice sweeps out the clutter of the god-pretentious self, making
ample space for Father, Son, and Holy Spirit; it embraces and prepares
for a kind of death that the culture knows nothing about,
making room for the dance of resurrection.

EUGENE PETERSON

The Monastery of Christ in the Desert sits at the end of a thirteen-mile "driveway" in a remote part of the mountainous desert of the Chama Canyon in the New Mexico badlands. It's one of the most beautiful places I've been in my life. You almost need a four-wheel-drive vehicle to make it up and down the rutted dirt road that leads to the home of a group of monks whose lives are ordered by the sixth-century Rule of St. Benedict. My family made it in our minivan.

We arrived in the middle of the day, just before midday prayer. The monk in charge of welcoming guests greeted us warmly. But in the midst of our conversation the bell began to ring, signaling the call for the monks to set aside their work and gather in the chapel for what Benedict called the *Opus Dei*, the work of God. Our host quickly invited us to join the monks for their time of prayer and then scurried off to join the others who were beginning to assemble.

The beautiful chapel, designed by the Japanese-American architect George Nakashima, looks as though it's been carved out of the side of the sandstone cliff that rises high above the back wall. We entered to find a simple but elegant cross-shaped sanctuary, took our places in the rough-hewn wooden pews and watched as the monks entered in their long robes and hoods covering the tops of their heads. They sat in two groups on opposite sides of the chapel and after a few minutes began to sing their prayers.

Benedict's rule carefully defines the rhythms of prayer and work that Benedictine monks and nuns around the world have followed for fifteen hundred years. Seven times a day they gather in the chapel to pray, primarily through singing the Psalms. My family sat listening as the voices reverberated through air. After they finished their singing, the monks bowed for an extended period of silence. It was in this holy moment that my eighteen-month-old daughter discovered that her voice could also echo through the chapel. She began cooing and squawking, making happy baby sounds at the top of her lungs. Mortified by her intrusion into their sacred silence and the complete ineffectiveness of my attempts to quiet her down, I looked over toward the place where the abbot was seated. He raised his hooded head from his posture of prayer and, to my relief, revealed a huge smile from ear to ear. My guess is that it wasn't very often the Benedictines heard baby sounds in their chapel.

The monks of Christ in the Desert live lives of rigorous spiritual discipline. And while it might seem that they have mastered "life with

God" but abandoned "for the world," it is worth noting that the Benedictine tradition is largely responsible for education as we know it through their libraries and their founding of schools. They are responsible for healthcare as we know it through their tradition of providing medical care to their neighbors and establishing some of the earliest hospitals. They provided the first hostels where weary travelers could find food to eat and a safe place to sleep. They have contributed significantly to the development of art, architecture, literature and just and sustainable economic development. It was the form of life embraced by these monastic communities that was largely responsible for sustaining the life of the mind and a spirituality of the heart through the so-called dark ages of the medieval era.

In recent years a number of books have been published that attempt to offer insights from the monastic life to those of us who live outside the cloister, exploring what it might look like to live into the patterns of prayer, work, rest and community that are at the heart of Benedictine spirituality. My own study of and experience with Benedictine monasticism has left me with a deep appreciation of their way of life and a deep longing to have my life in the world shaped by the rhythms that shape and sustain them.

Whether we live in a remote monastery, the heart of a large city or anywhere in between, we need a set of practices and patterns for living—a rule of life—that will shape and sustain our life with God for the world. We need practices that nurture our souls and enable us to increasingly inhabit the vision of God in the places where we dwell— to live into the story of the Bible, the story of God's personal presence, just reign and perfect peace. These will be practices that demand things of us. They will require our disciplined attention and engagement. These will be practices that connect us to one another. They will help us live life together as a contrast community, against the world for the sake of the world. These practices will connect us to a tradition. They will have a rich heritage from the Christian past, having shaped and sustained the people of God for a long time. Finally, these will be practices that orient us toward the future. They will help us inhabit the vision of God in the particular places where we dwell. I will talk about specific practices in the subsequent chapters, but first we need to consider some characteristics common to our practice of all of the disciplines.

Learning Grammar

In this chapter I want to provide a "grammar" of the spiritual disciplines. A grammar is not the employment of a language itself, it is the substructure of the language that "makes it work." If we want to do things with words, we need a grammar to put them together to accomplish our intentions. A grammar of the spiritual disciplines then refers not so much to the practices themselves as to the substructure of the practices, the ways in which they are appropriately engaged. So in this chapter I want to highlight five characteristics that are a part of the skillful engagement in the spiritual disciplines.

But first I need to offer two important caveats. First, many people skillfully employ language without ever learning all the details of grammar. In fact, the way we learn a language is usually not by beginning with a grammar lesson but by following the examples of accomplished language users and imitating them. Anyone who has watched a young child learning to talk has seen this play out. We learn by imitation and practice. So too with the spiritual disciplines. We need not learn a "grammar" to pray. We learn to pray by praying, and often we best learn to pray by following the example of experienced prayers. In their book *Resident Aliens*, Stanley Hauerwas and William Willimon employ the same language metaphor in their discussion of "learning to be moral." They make the point by saying, "You learn to speak by being initiated into a community of language, by observing your elders, by imitating them. The rules of grammar come later, if at all, as a way of enabling you to nourish and sustain the art of speaking well."[1]

Second, learning this grammar of the disciplines is about more than effective technique. Knowing the grammar—the substructure—of the spiritual disciplines does not mean that doing them "right" implies that they'll automatically "work." We go wrong in our thinking about the spiritual disciplines if we think of them in this mechanical way. We want a formula, a calculus. We want certainty and control. We're habituated into thinking that if we apply the right means we'll achieve our desired ends. But such thinking ends up turning the spiritual disciplines into the means by which we transform ourselves or manipulate God, neither of which is desirable or possible. As I have insisted throughout, the Holy Spirit accomplishes our transformation and he is neither limited by nor beholden to these particular means. We cannot manipulate the Holy Spirit by our engagement in these practices. As Richard Foster has said, "the Spiritual Disciplines in and of themselves have no merit whatsoever. They possess no righteousness, contain no rectitude. Their purpose—their only purpose—is to place us before God. After that they have come to the end of their tether. But it is enough."[2]

The grammar I want to offer in this chapter is captured in five words. These five words, I believe, characterize the devotional lives that we see on display or that are commended to us in the Bible. They characterize the way in which the holy men and women of the church's history have engaged God. They would easily be observed if you made the trek to Christ in the Desert. But they are also evident in the lives of everyday saints who surround us every time the church gathers. It should also be said that each of these five elements of our grammar is deeply complicated by the kind of cultural environment in which we find ourselves. Each element is, in a sense, countercultural. If we are to live life with God for the world—to practice the vision in our everyday lives—we need to engage this countercultural grammar. The five words that make up our grammar are attentiveness, receptivity, embodiment, community and rhythm.

Attentiveness

After sharing the Last Supper together, Jesus and his friends made the trek from the upper room down through the Kidron Valley and up the side of the Mount of Olives to the Garden of Gethsemane. Somewhere along that ancient pathway Jesus introduced his disciples to what has become a famous metaphor for the spiritual life: "I am the vine, you are the branches. Those who abide in me and I in them bear much fruit, because apart from me you can do nothing" (John 15:5 NRSV). Perhaps as they walked along they passed the entrance to a vineyard. Or maybe Jesus caught a glimpse in the moonlight of the golden vine and its fruit adorning the gates of the temple. Whatever the inspiration, Jesus seized on an important image of life lived in vital connection with him. As he reinforced the metaphor throughout his short teaching, he repeated over and over—eleven times in the space of seventeen verses—the call to abide in him. The metaphor implies a sense of intimate relationship and life-giving dependence that is the essence of the spiritual life. But like all metaphors, this one obscures even as it reveals. What does it mean to abide in Christ? How does that work out in our overly complicated, twenty-first-century lives? I'd like to suggest that at least one crucial aspect of what it means to abide in Christ—an aspect that is fundamental to the proper practice of all spiritual disciplines—is paying attention.

One of the most important spiritual capacities we can develop in a world like ours is the capacity to pay attention. In our contemporary cultural environment we suffer from a kind of collective attention deficit disorder. The ability to give sustained attention to people, to ideas and to the state of our own souls is absolutely indispensable to the cultivation of intimacy in relationships, depth of understanding and wisdom for life. Thus the erosion of our ability to pay attention is no small matter. We are increasingly becoming an easily distractible people living in an increasingly distracting world. The ubiquity of technology, the breakneck pace of life and the invasiveness of "productivity" into every sphere of our existence have demolished our old conceptions of place, time and space and have dismantled our ability to achieve sustained focus, deep awareness, thoughtful reflection and vibrant memory. Yet these capacities are indispensable for anything more than a superficial spirituality (not to mention family life, friendship, political community and so on). In her book *Distracted: The Erosion of Attention and the Coming Dark Age*, Maggie Jackson goes so far as to argue, "The waning of our powers of attention is occurring at such a rate and in so many areas of life, that the erosion is reaching critical mass. We are on the verge of losing our capacity as a society for deep, sustained focus. In short, we are slipping toward a new dark age."[3] The cultural consequences of our collective loss of attentiveness could be significant indeed.

Leighton Ford has observed, "From the time we were children we were told to 'pay attention,' as if this were the simplest thing in the world. But in fact attentiveness is one of the most difficult concepts to grasp and one of the hardest disciplines to learn."[4] Attentiveness is one of the essential constitutive components of the spiritual disciplines. The spiritual disciplines are, at their most basic, means by which we pay attention. They are intentional practices of sustained focus—on God, on his story, on our neighbors and on the condition of our own souls. They involve carving out space in the midst of our daily lives to call our souls to attentiveness, to lift our eyes from the innumerable distractions that vie for our loyalty and affections.

First, we must learn to be attentive to God, to the reality of his presence and our need of him. One of the most significant aspects of a spiritual discipline is that it wakes us to the oft-neglected reality that the Spirit is present with us, that he desires to do his work in us, that he longs for us to experience his formative and sustaining power in our souls. Walking by the Spirit—abiding in Christ—begins with the acknowledgment, "God, in this moment, you are with me and I am with you." Spiritual disciplines are the means by which we carve out space in our overbusy, easily preoccupied lives to practice the presence of God.

Second, we need practices that help us be attentive to the story, attentive to the vision of God. The particular practices I will explore in subsequent chapters are all means of helping us come back to the vision of God—God's personal presence, God's just reign and God's perfect peace—time and time again. Inhabiting this story requires immersion in the story. We live in an environment filled with other competing stories that hold out a vision of the good life. For example, every television commercial is a thirty-second "beatitude," a story of what the "blessed life" looks like—and it's inevitably tied to a consumer product. We are surrounded by stories. We need practices that draw our attention back to the story that, for us, trumps all others.

Third, we need practices that will help us be attentive to what's going on in the world around us. Often our spiritual disciplines are practices that cause us to bow our heads in focused attention to God and the soul. As crucial as that may be, we also need practices that help us lift our heads to see the reality going on around us. In his book *The Inward Journey*, theologian and civil rights pioneer Howard Thurman claims that it is the duty of Christian spirituality to "keep a troubled vigil at the bedside of the world."[5]

Finally, we need those practices that help us pay attention to the reality and condition of our own souls. Spirituality takes the soul seriously. The soul is "the invisibility that inheres in every visibility, . . . the interior that provides content to every exterior."[6] But given our penchant for living increasingly distracted lives in an increasingly distracting culture, we can manage to move through life failing to notice that we have a soul, that it needs nurture, that it requires care. Spiritual disciplines carve out space to pay attention to the soul.

Receptivity

A few days before his death, Martin Luther took up his pen and wrote what would be the final lines of a prolific writing life: "We are all beggars, this is true." These last words are an appropriate epitaph for a man whose singular devotion to the gospel of grace changed the face of Western history. They echo the words of Jesus that are the starting point of his teaching on discipleship: "Blessed are the poor in spirit, for theirs is the kingdom of heaven" (Matthew 5:3). Spirituality in the way of Jesus begins with the recognition of our own inadequacy, the acknowledgment of our own spiritual bankruptcy. It is only here that we encounter the transforming power of grace. Tragically, grace is viewed by many merely as a description of God's favor given to us in the moment of our salvation. In this view grace is narrowly associated with justification and confined to the beginning of the Christian life. But as Jim Wilhoit points out, "There are over one hundred references to grace in the English New Testament, and fewer than 10 percent of these refer principally to justification. Grace has much to do with how we live. For too many people, grace is about how we are 'saved' and work is about how we 'grow.' Yet the New Testament is clear that grace is God's merciful and restoring power as well."[7] Divine grace is not merely the means of our salvation but the power of our transformation in the Christian life.

This recognition helps guard against a fundamental misunderstanding of the spiritual disciplines. The practices of the spiritual life commended to us in Scripture and developed through the history of the church are not the means by which we transform ourselves. They are the means by which the Holy Spirit graciously works to transform us into the image of Jesus. Our engagement in the historical disciplines is an intentional response to God's grace through a divinely appointed means of grace that enables us to encounter the transforming power of grace. In engaging the disciplines, we engage in a deliberate decentering of the self. As James Kushiner rightly suggests, "A discipline won't bring you closer to God. Only God can bring you closer to Himself. What the discipline is meant to do is to help you get yourself, your ego, out of the way so you are open to His grace."[8]

First, spiritual disciplines are a response to grace. God has made the prior gesture. We do not experience spiritual growth by trying harder. We experience spiritual growth when we respond to the kindness God has lavished on us in Jesus by availing ourselves to the Spirit, letting him do what he wants to do in us that we can't do for ourselves. And importantly, even that response is itself grace. In Philippians Paul writes, "Continue to work out your salvation with fear and trembling, for it is God who works in you to will and to act in order to fulfill his good purpose" (Philippians 2:12-13). Here Paul speaks in the imperative: there is a "working out" that we're called to do. But he quickly adds that it is only by God's work in us that we are capable of willing and acting to accomplish his purpose. Spiritual disciplines are a response to grace.

Second, spiritual disciplines are a means of grace. The Holy Spirit is the "fountain of living water," according to Jesus. As C. S. Lewis's metaphor that opened this chapter indicates, spiritual disciplines are simply those practices that put us in a position to get wet. The classical spiritual disciplines are formative practices that have been commended to us in Scripture and developed through the history of the church that are God's own appointed means for accomplishing his intention in our lives. They are the ways we carve our space and open our souls to the Spirit's work of grace.

Finally, as we respond to grace through the means of grace we experience the transforming power of grace. The Spirit's intention in each of our lives is to conform us to the image of Jesus, to refine us, liberating us from the power of the soul turned in upon itself and enabling us to make the outward turn toward God and others. This outward turn is the transformation Christian spirituality pursues. It happens by the power of the Spirit at work in us as we open ourselves to receive what he has to offer. "We are all beggars, that is true."

③ Embodiment

One of the most pernicious of the early threats to orthodox Christianity was the heresy of Docetism. The name of this particular heresy comes from the Greek word *dokeo*, which means "to seem." The Docetists insisted that Jesus only seemed to have a body. In their view, Jesus' divinity made it impossible for him to have possessed a body of flesh and blood. To be embodied was an imperfection, a limitation, a weakness that would mean he was capable of suffering. Surely the divine could not have a body, could not really dwell among us in the flesh, could not really suffer with us and for us.

Docetism was explicitly rejected at the council of Nicaea in A.D. 325. It has been considered outside the bounds of Christian orthodoxy ever since. Docetism in its historical form doesn't appear to be a great threat to Christianity in our day. But I'm beginning to wonder if we might be in danger of a different kind of Docetism in the church today, a docetic spirituality in which we human beings only seem to have a body. In other words, are we developing ways of thinking about the spiritual life and ways of being in the world that make our bodies merely ancillary?

My office at the seminary is on the corner of Live Oak and St. Joseph, just on the edge of downtown Dallas. Every day when I get in my car to head home I drive west on Live Oak toward the heart of the city. Several months ago a new feature on the urban landscape interrupted the monotony of my daily commute. One of the tall downtown buildings had become a billboard. Its drab gray side had been covered over with an enormous advertisement.

Its size and prominence on the downtown skyline certainly caught my attention. But I was even more taken in by its message. In large red letters written across the center of the ad space was the message "Closeness has nothing to do with distance." Surrounding the declaration were images of smartphones. It was a colossal advertisement for Blackberry, declaring the good news that, thanks to the grace of technology, physical proximity is now irrelevant to personal relationships. With technology this effective, our bodies really don't matter.

As I drove on, I thought for awhile about the gospel according to Blackberry. My mind went back to a conversation I'd had with a friend just a few weeks before. My friend had recently walked through the heartache of losing her father, but the tears in her eyes on this occasion weren't about her grief over his death. She was grieving over the painful fiction that "closeness has nothing to do with distance." As she wiped a tear from her cheek she told me, "I got beautiful email messages, and beautiful Facebook messages, and beautiful voicemail messages, and beautiful text messages. But nobody just came and sat with me and cried with me." As I thought about that conversation, I realized that despite modern technology's evangelistic proclamations to the contrary, technology can never fully replace the power of presence. Bodies matter.

In the first chapter I suggested that Christian spirituality is body affirming. Our bodies are a crucial aspect of our humanity. They are a part of God's good creation. We bear his image in the world as embodied creatures. And our hope as Christians is an embodied hope. We're not waiting merely to be liberated from our bodies but for the resurrection of our bodies and the renewal of all creation. From the garden to the city, our bodies matter. And in between the garden and the city, we find the spiritual life of the people of God—in both the Old and New Testaments—shaped by their participation in embodied practices. What we do with our bodies matters to our souls. Body postures such as standing, kneeling and bowing are not arbitrary. Body rituals such as fasting and feasting are a regular part of the formation of God's people. While the Bible certainly emphasizes the interior dispositions of the heart when it comes to "practicing our righteousness" (see Matthew 6:1-18), it does not thereby negate the significance of our bodies.

A spirituality that is deeply informed by the logic of the incarnation means treating our bodies with as much seriousness as we treat our souls. As James K. A. Smith has perceptively written,

> Taking the incarnation seriously means taking bodies seriously, which means affirming the space that they occupy as an arena of revelation and grace. The sacramental imagination begins from the assumption that our discipleship depends not only—not even primarily—on the conveyance of ideas into our minds, but on our immersion in embodied practices and rituals that form us into the kind of people God calls us to be. . . . For we embodied creatures, whether ancient or postmodern, the rhythms of ritual and liturgy are gracious practices that enable discipleship and formation."[9]

Our bodies are not ancillary when it comes to Christian spirituality. To have a body is the essence of what it means to be human. What we do with our bodies matters to our souls.

 ## Community

The Protestant Reformation often gets either the praise or the blame for the "advent of the individual." It's not that there were no individual persons prior to the Reformation, but the understanding of what it meant to be human and what it meant to relate to God was understood in much more communal ways before the sixteenth century. The Reformation brought attention to the state of the individual soul before God. Theologian Karl Heim identified this individualizing impulse as the "first principle of Protestantism," namely, that a person meets God "only in a spiritual act that occurs in deep solitude and with full mental clarity."[10] This spiritual act occurs "entirely alone and independent of all other men."[11] Heim captures the same sentiment as the German church historian Adolf von Harnack, who insists, "The kingdom of God comes by coming to the individual, by entering into his soul and laying hold of it. . . . It is not a question . . . of thrones and principalities, but of God and the soul, the soul and its God."[12]

While the individualizing impulse of the Reformation may have contributed to the rise of modern individualism, the caricatures portrayed by Heim and Harnack simply don't square with what the Reformers themselves taught. For example, Calvin highlights the essential function of the community of faith when he unpacks his favorite metaphor for the church, the church as "mother of all the godly." He writes,

> Let us learn even from the simple title "mother" how useful, indeed how necessary, it is that we should know her. For there is no other way to enter into life unless this mother conceive us in her womb, give us birth, nourish us at her breast, and lastly, unless she keep us under her care and guidance until, putting off mortal flesh, we become like the angels.[13]

Calvin can go so far as to say, "Away from her bosom one cannot hope for any forgiveness of sins or any salvation."[14]

This venture into church history highlights just how far many Christians today—heirs of the Protestant Reformation—have come from the historical view of the place of the church in the spiritual life. The church, as I suggested in chapter three, is the dwelling place of God. The church is not a religious goods and services provider that is at times a helpful supplement to my private pursuit of God. The church is "the mother of all the godly."

This understanding of the church—as depicted in the Bible and expressed in the church's rich history—runs counter to the strong individualism that so pervades our contemporary Western cultural environment. Because the pervasive understanding of salvation in North American Christianity tends to focus so narrowly on one's personal relationship with Jesus, our understanding of the Christian life tends to focus narrowly on one's own individual spiritual journey. But this reflects a way of thinking and being in the world that is more

American than Christian. As Joseph Hellerman has said,

> We must embrace the fact that our value system has been shaped
> by a worldview that is diametrically opposed to the outlook of the
> early Christians and to the teachings of Scripture. As church-going
> Americans, we have been socialized to believe that our individual
> fulfillment and our personal relationship with God are more im-
> portant than any connection we might have with our fellow human
> beings, whether in the home or in the church. We have, in a most
> subtle and insidious way, been conformed to this world.[15]

The church in North America desperately needs to recover a robust
understanding of what it means to be the church.

The significance of all of this for our thinking about the spiritual
disciplines is found in recognizing that the spiritual disciplines are the
formative practices of the church. We ought not think of them primarily in terms of private spiritual practices that help *me* shape and
sustain *my* life with God but as the church's practices that help *us*
shape and sustain *our* lives with God. This way of thinking causes us
to consider how we can engage in formative practice together as the
community gathered. As will be discussed further in chapter seven,
the practices embedded in the church's weekly gathering for worship
are among the most formative spiritual disciplines we engage, even if
we fail to pay attention to them as "formative" or as "spiritual disciplines." Understanding the spiritual disciplines as the community's
formative practices also emphasizes how my own personal practice of
the disciplines is an extension of the life and practice of the community. It ought to be the church that teaches me the disciplines, the
church that encourages me in the disciplines, and the building up of
the church that is the aim of my practice of the disciplines as I learn
to do alone what we do together. One's personal practice of Christian
spirituality is recognizable and intelligible only to the extent that it is
an extension of church's form of life and practice.

① attentiveness ② receptivity ③ embodiment
A Grammar of the Disciplines 115
④ community

Rhythm

The final aspect of our grammar of the spiritual disciplines is rhythm. In both the Old and New Testaments, the lives of God's people were shaped by a particular set of rhythms. There was for them a rhythm of the day, a rhythm of the week and a rhythm of the year. Daily, their lives were marked by prayers and recitations at appointed times. Every pious Israelite would recite the Shema at least twice every day, as the day began and as it came to an end: "Hear, O Israel: The LORD our God, the LORD is one. Love the LORD your God with all your heart and with all your soul and with all your strength" (Deuteronomy 6:4-5). Weekly, the lives of the people of God have been shaped by established patterns of work, rest and worship. Israel's weekly rhythm of life was distinct from the surrounding world, as they lived into the story of the work and rest of God in the biblical account of creation. Yearly, the lives of Old Testament believers were formed by their inhabiting the stories of the mighty deeds of God in the great festivals that commemorated his saving work in the exodus from Egypt, the giving of the Law at Sinai, the miraculous provision in the wilderness, and the ongoing provision demonstrated by the firstfruits of the annual harvest. This liturgical calendar of Israel was a communal, embodied set of rhythms of remembrance.

In the early centuries of the Christian era, these rhythms of the day, week and year began to take on a distinctly Christian character. Over time the daily recitation of the Shema was replaced by the daily recitation of the Lord's Prayer. The young church eventually came to shift its day of rest and worship to the first day of the week to commemorate the new creation that began with the resurrection of Jesus on the very first Easter. The great festivals of the Jewish calendar were exchanged for the seasons of Advent, Epiphany, Lent, Easter and Pentecost—rhythms of remembrance centered in the life story of Jesus and God's mighty deeds of salvation through him.

Many Christians today suffer from a kind of "collective arrhythmia."[16]

We have so prized freedom and spontaneity that we have lost the rich formative significance of rhythm and ritual. This is complicated by the fact that many people who grew up in Christian traditions that maintained the church's historical rhythms suffered from a disconnect between ritual and meaning. I know many Christians who only much later in life have come to understand and appreciate the richness of the rituals they participated in during their younger years. And I know many others who now want nothing to do with formal ritual precisely because they found it so lifeless.

Jesus warned against the emptiness of what the King James Version called "vain repetition" (Matthew 6:7). But, sadly, this has caused many evangelical Christians to think of all repetition as vain repetition. Part of human learning and formation is participation in repeated practices that form habits of life down deep in our bones. As Stanley Hauerwas and William Willimon have said,

> Most of the really important things we do in life, we do out of habit. We eat, sleep, make love, shake hands, hug our children out of habit. Some things in life are too difficult to be left up to spontaneous desire—things like telling people that we love them or praying to God. So we do them "out of habit." Thus, in the church we generally do the same things over and over again, week after week, telling the same stories and singing the same songs.[17]

Not all repetition is vain repetition. The issue that Jesus had in view is the disposition of the heart. In the Old Testament, God's people were expected to engage in daily, weekly and yearly formative rhythms with a heart of gratitude and expectation. These same formative rhythms would have shaped and sustained the lives of Jesus and his first followers. Over time, the specific rhythms shifted to center on the person and work of Jesus. But God's means of shaping and sustaining the lives of his people has always been through formation by rhythm.

The disciplines of the Christian life have been commended to us in Scripture and passed on to us through the history of the church. They are not the means by which we accomplish our own work of transformation but the means by which we position ourselves before the Spirit and allow him to do his work in us. The chapters ahead point to a handful of selected disciplines that nurture and sustain our life with God for the world. But we will begin at the beginning, with the practice that holds pride of place, the practice of prayer.

6

Let It Be

Practicing the Vision in Prayer

To clasp the hands in prayer is the beginning of
an uprising against the disorder of the world.

KARL BARTH

Prayer is the highest use to which speech can be put.
It is the highest meaning that can be put into words.

P. T. FORSYTH

According to Kierkegaard, "True prayer is a struggle with God, in which one triumphs through the victory of God."[1] Since I first encountered this line, I've taken great comfort in knowing that struggle is somehow of the essence of prayer. I have certainly always found prayer a struggle. I've struggled with how to pray. I've struggled with questions about the efficacy of prayer. I've struggled with the ways God has answered (or apparently not answered) my prayers. But most of all I've simply struggled to pray. Prayer is a struggle, but as Kierkegaard rightly points out, it is a struggle with God. To speak of practices that shape and sustain our life with God for the world is to speak first and foremost of prayer. Prayer is "the central avenue God uses to transform us."[2] As the eighteenth-century devotional writer William Law has said, "Prayer is the nearest approach to God and the highest enjoyment of Him that we are capable of in this life. It is the noblest exercise of the soul, the most exalted use of our best faculties, and the highest imitation of the blessed inhabitants of Heaven."[3] Prayer is the central practice of the with-God life.

The Primacy of Prayer

Prayer holds a certain pride of place among the spiritual disciplines because it is in an important sense the practice on which all the other disciplines depend. In prayer we posture ourselves before and address God directly. The other disciplines are either a preparation for, a means of or an accompaniment to prayer. Silence and solitude are means by which we keep out the noise and distractions of the world around us so we are able to pay attention to God and open ourselves to his work in prayer. Meditation on Scripture is undertaken in a posture of prayer and as a preparation for prayer. Fasting is a bodily discipline that accompanies prayer and serves as an aid to prayer as our physical hunger reminds us of our dependence on God and leads us to cry out to him. Prayer holds primacy among the spiritual disciplines because each of the others is vitally connected to it.

In addition, prayer holds a place of preeminence because it is the practice we come by most naturally. It is "the *lingua franca* of the human heart."[4] As Anne Lamott has suggested, all prayer basically comes down to one of three types: "Help me! Help me! Help me!" "Thank you! Thank you! Thank you!" and "Wow!"[5] Human beings have a natural inclination to appeal to a power beyond themselves for help in times of need. We have an innate sense of gratitude for the good that comes to us in life and are in search of one to whom we can give thanks. And we inevitably find ourselves in awe of the beauty we encounter in the world and want to offer praise to the source of the beauty that moves us so deeply. The Christian story names for us the one who is our "ever present help in times of trouble," the one who is "the giver of all good gifts," and the one who is "the maker of heaven and earth." In prayer, we voice these primal sentiments of our souls to the God we've come to know and trust in Jesus. As Simon Chan has said, "Prayers are the life signs of faith. They occur as naturally as the cries of newborn babies."[6]

The Difficulty of Prayer

But to say that prayer is natural should not be confused with saying that prayer is easy. For some of us it can be exceedingly difficult. I've always found it incredibly reassuring to see that the disciples came to Jesus and said, "Lord, teach us to pray" (Luke 11:1). These were grown men, pious Jews who had no doubt been praying their entire lives. But in their approach to Jesus they acknowledged that they were mere beginners when it came to knowing how to pray. In their book *Living the Story: Biblical Spirituality for Everyday Christians*, Paul Stevens and Michael Green write, "Prayer is difficult. A few giants of the faith say that prayer is as normal to them as breathing. But most of us find that prayer is like any other form of relational communion—it takes constant effort."[7] As with other forms of "relational communion," prayer is difficult for at least four reasons.

First, prayer is difficult because it requires attentiveness. As I suggested in the last chapter, the capacity to pay attention is one of the most important spiritual capacities we can develop in the world we're living in. Prayer is paying attention to God. But as easily distracted people in an increasingly distracting world, paying attention to God is complicated. Indeed, paying attention to anything is complicated. One of the main reasons we find prayer difficult in our cultural environment is that it demands that we be attentive, that we focus in the midst of all the busyness, noise and distraction of our complex lives. But like any other form of relational communion, the attention we give to the other (or, in this case, the Other) is the foundation on which intimacy, understanding and trust are built.

Second, prayer is difficult because it requires a decentering of the self. If prayer is paying attention to God, it requires us to take the attention off of ourselves. Christian philosopher Merold Westphal suggests that the most important element of prayer is also the most difficult, namely, the element of praise. Praise is that element of prayer that is "not concerned with benefits for me or those I care about." In praise, Westphal says, "we have that disinterested delight (to cite Evelyn Underhill) in the bare goodness of God (to cite Luther) that escapes the self's preoccupation with the self."[8] Authentic Christian prayer stabs at the flesh, the outlook oriented toward the self. Though we often approach prayer as a useful strategy for getting what we want, the biblical vision of prayer is about learning to bend our wants to what God wants. We need to take the posture of beginners at prayer and be taught to pray, because left to our own devices our prayers will be too much about us. The flourishing of any form of relational communion requires us to move beyond "the self's preoccupation with the self." This is every bit as true of our friendship with God is it is of any other friendship we have.

Third, we find prayer difficult because it requires honesty. Achieving intimacy in any relationship requires us to move beyond pretense and image management and to really be honest with the other. We have to give up on the hope of manipulating the actions and affections of the other by saying all the right things at the right times in the right ways. We have to be real.

Not long ago I got a call from a childhood friend that led to one of the most tender conversations about prayer I've ever had. She and I have been friends for more than three decades, but she has been a follower of Jesus for only a couple of years. She called with a question she was embarrassed to ask but that she couldn't escape: "Is there a right way and a wrong way to pray?" Behind the question was personal pain born of her ongoing struggle with infertility. What she really wanted to know was, "Is God not answering my prayers because I'm not doing it right? If I did things differently, could I know he'd listen and respond?" As we talked, I got to hear the ache of her soul in her longing for a child and the ache that came from her struggle to make sense of it all in light of her newfound faith. The main thing I tried to tell her that day is that God invites us to be honest with him in our prayers, that God wants us to pray as we are and not as we should be. We talked about how the Bible not only gives us permission but even models for us in the psalms of lament how to express ourselves honestly before God even when that honesty involves confusion, pain and disappointment with God himself. As Gerald Sittser notes, "Surprisingly, God seems to look with compassion and favor on those who accuse him and yell at him. . . . What God can't tolerate is a plastic saint, a polite believer, someone who plays a part but never gets inside the soul of the character. God prefers working with people who like to fight."[9] God wants us to abandon pretense and our feeble attempts at manipulation and to be honest with him in prayer.

Finally, prayer—like other forms of relational communion—is difficult because it requires trust. And to trust is to be vulnerable. According to Donald Bloesch, "Christian prayer is born out of the realization that human beings in and of themselves are incapable of saving themselves from the forces of darkness within and about them. In genuine prayer, we come to God with empty hands trusting solely in his mercy."[10] But this kind of vulnerable trust doesn't come easily to those of us who have learned by culture and experience to trust no one. And some of us have trusted God in prayer only to find ourselves feeling deeply disappointed with the results.

I've often pondered the story told in Acts 12 of the apostle Peter's miraculous escape from prison. When Peter shows up at the doorstep of the people who are gathered to pray for his release, they're completely incredulous. Despite praying for his release, they can't believe it's really him. When they realize that God has answered their prayers and that he is really there, they are "astonished" (Acts 12:16). The thing I've always found baffling about this story is not the miraculous getaway or the incredulity of the disciples gathered for prayer. It's the words that set the context for the whole story: "It was about this time that King Herod arrested some who belonged to the church, intending to persecute them. He had James, the brother of John, put to death with the sword" (Acts 12:1-2). I have to think that the same group of Christ-followers gathered and prayed every bit as earnestly for James as they did for Peter. But the outcome of the story for each of these men who had been Jesus' closest companions was very different. Why was Peter set free by the hand of God and James allowed to die? The text doesn't give us any inkling of an answer. We're left with little to say but to observe that God is faithful but not predictable. He invites us to pray, trusting his faithfulness, even when we struggle to discern how he is faithful in all the details of our lives; trusting that his faithfulness will prevail in the larger story he is writing with each of our lives.

Lord, Teach Us to Pray

Something about watching Jesus at prayer made his disciples feel as though they were mere novices. According to Luke's Gospel, one of the disciples approached him after he had finished his own time with the Father and said to him, "Lord, teach us to pray, just as John taught his disciples" (Luke 11:1). Evidently Jesus' disciples were aware that John the Baptist had instructed his disciples in the practice of prayer, perhaps having given them a prayer to make their own. What follows is Luke's account of what we've come to refer to as "the Lord's Prayer."

Not long ago I was a part of a discussion with a number of other Christian leaders where we were busy planning an upcoming gathering in which each of us would be participating. Since the subject at the center of the gathering was prayer, someone suggested that we recite the Lord's Prayer together as part of the service. One of the members of the group spoke up: "I hate it when we recite the Lord's Prayer in unison. It just seems inauthentic. After all, Jesus didn't say 'Pray these words,' but 'Pray in this way.'"

A bit taken aback by this protest, my mind immediately went to Luke 11. While my friend's "in this way" may reflect Jesus' manner of speaking in the more well-known account of Matthew 6, in Luke 11:2 Jesus actually says, "When you pray, say . . . " As Luke records things, Jesus intended to give his disciples not only a pattern to follow in prayer but the actual words to pray to God. He gives them his prayer, which is to become theirs. One of the earliest Christian documents outside of the New Testament is a discipleship manual known to scholars as the *Didache*. According to the instruction of the *Didache*, the early followers of Jesus were to pray the Lord's Prayer three times every day. It was for them a fundamental part of the rhythm of life.

However, while my friend may have been off base in his strong bias against corporate recitation of the Lord's Prayer, he was correct to note that it is a profoundly instructive model for prayer. It teaches us what really matters in prayer, what really matters to God and ought ultimately to matter to us. And what we find in the prayer is that what really matters covers a tremendous span, from the greatest of things (God's name, God's kingdom) to the smallest things (our daily bread). As both our words of prayer and our model of prayer, the Lord's Prayer has great potential to transform those of us who pray it even as we pray for God to transform the world. As Simone Weil has said, "The Our Father contains all possible petitions; we cannot conceive of any prayer not already contained in it. It is to prayer what Christ is to humanity. It is impossible to say it once through, giving the fullest possible attention to each word, without a change, infinitesimal but real, taking place in the soul."[11] In what follows, I want to unpack this prayer in a way that informs both our use of the prayer itself as well as our priorities in prayer even when we're not using these words themselves.

"Our"

The first thing to note about the prayer is that it is inescapably communal. Even to pray this prayer in private is to pray a corporate prayer, for we do not address God as "my Father," but "our Father." We do not pray for "my daily bread," but "our daily bread." As Karl Barth suggests, "It presupposes 'us.'"[12] This "us," says Barth, is created by Jesus' invitation to follow him. This is the "Disciples' Prayer" as much as it is the "Lord's Prayer." In praying this prayer we are taught to pray not as individuals but as the community of disciples, as the church. But in an important sense, it is a prayer of the disciples in solidarity with those who do not yet pray. Barth writes, "When Christians pray, they are, so to speak, the substitutes for all those who do not pray; and in this sense they are in communion with them in the same manner as Jesus Christ has entered into solidarity with sinners, with a lost human race."[13] To pray this prayer is to pray with the church for the world.

With this understanding in mind, we also need to recognize that praying this prayer obliges us to act on behalf of those with whom and for whom we pray. As P. T. Forsyth has said, "A prayer is also a promise. Every true prayer carries with it a vow. If it does not, it is not in earnest. It is not of a piece with life. Can we pray in earnest if we do not in the act commit ourselves to do our best to bring about the answer?"[14] If we pray to God sincerely, we must be willing to allow God to use us to bring about the answer to our prayer. Forsyth continues:

> Prayer is one form of sacrifice, but if it is the only form it is vain oblation. If we pray for our child that he may have God's blessing, we are really promising that nothing shall be lacking on our part to be a divine blessing to him. And if we have no kind of religious relation to him (as plenty of Christian parents have none), our prayer is quite unreal, and its failure should not be a surprise. To pray for God's kingdom is also to engage ourselves to service and sacrifice for it. To begin our prayer with a petition for the hal-

lowing of God's name and to have no real and prime place for holiness in our life or faith is not sincere.[15]

The things for which we pray are beyond our ability to obtain in our own power. That is why we pray. To even begin to pray is to acknowledge our need of God. But to pray in earnest is to commit to availing ourselves to God as the means through which he may choose, in part, to bring about its answer.

"Our Father"

There are several things we should note about the invitation of Jesus to address God as "our Father." The first has to do with our adoption as daughters and sons and the astonishing privilege into which Jesus invites us. We will not feel the power of the prayer if we fail to recognize that we have no right in and of ourselves to call him "Father." We have the incredible privilege to address him in this manner only because of the decisive work of Jesus, the Son. "We are his children, he is our Father, by virtue of this new birth realized at Christmas, on Good Friday, at Easter and fulfilled at the moment of our baptism."[16] It is Jesus, the Son, who makes us into his brothers and sisters and invites us to address God as Father. This is the fundamental reason we address our prayers to the Father "through Christ, our Lord" (or "in Jesus' name"). It is only through the work of the Son on our behalf that we have the confidence of being heard by a benevolent Father in heaven. Jesus gives us the privilege of addressing the king of the universe with the tender word a young child would use to affectionately address her father.

Second, to call God "Father" is not only a privilege of intimacy but also a declaration of longing and hope. It is, as N. T. Wright has suggested, a word of "revolution."[17] The first occurrence in the Old Testament of the idea of God as Father shows up when Moses defiantly speaks to the tyrant Pharaoh of Egypt, saying, "This is what the LORD says: 'Israel is my firstborn son, and I told you, "Let my son go, so he may worship me." But you refused to let him go'" (Exodus 4:22-23). For Israel to call God "Father" was to cling to the hope of liberty and deliverance from the tyrants. This is the association with God as Father that would have been embedded in the consciousness of Jesus' first followers. Therefore, according to Wright, "When Jesus tells his disciples to call God 'Father,' then, those with ears to hear will understand. He wants us to get ready for the new Exodus. We are going to be free at last. This is the Advent hope, the hope of the coming Kingdom of God. The tyrant's grip is going to be broken, and we shall be free."[18] To call God "Father" is to long for liberation for ourselves and for the world from the tyranny of sin and death.

This insight relates directly to the third important implication of calling God "Father." The other strong resonances Jesus' first hearers would have heard when they heard him address God as Father would have been messianic resonances. God had promised Israel a liberating king, a descendant of David who would rule God's people and whose kingdom would never end (see 2 Samuel 7:8-17; 1 Chronicles 17:11-14). Through the prophet Nathan, God said of this coming king, "I will be his father, and he will be my son" (2 Samuel 7:14). Over time Israel's hope in a coming new exodus and the promise of liberation came to be associated with their hope of the coming messianic king. Again, Wright's insights are helpful: "The two pictures go together. Freedom for Israel in bondage will come about through the liberating work of the Messiah. And Jesus, picking up all these resonances, is saying to his followers: this is your prayer. You are the liberty-people. You are the Messianic people."[19] To call God "Father" in the Lord's Prayer is to stake our claim as the people of the vision of God, the people of the dream of God for a world set right. We have been invited in by the Son, the Messiah, the one who taught us to pray, "Our Father . . ."

"Our Father in Heaven"

We're reminded when we pray to the Father that we address the God who is in heaven, the one who is sovereign over all his creation. He is, as the ancient creed declares, "the Father, the Almighty, maker of heaven and earth." As Hauerwas and Willimon have said, "Any less of a god wouldn't do us much good. The good that needs doing in this world—good for the poorest of the poor, the sickest of the sick, the most desperate of the desperate—tends to be considerably larger than our mere social activism, charity, or politics. Things are cosmically out of hand."[20] We need the help of the only one truly capable of helping us. We can be bold to pray for peace in the war-torn places, food to fill hungry stomachs, healing for the loved one with cancer, reconciliation in a strife-filled marriage or strength for faint hearts and feeble knees because we pray to the one "in heaven." And we can know that we always have an audience there, because he is "our Father in heaven." The one who is sovereign over the universe is so attentive to us as to know the number of hairs on our heads (see Matthew 10:30; Luke 12:7). There is no burden in our heart too great or too small to bring to the one who welcomes us and has the power to do something about it. To be a Christian who prays is to be a person "out of control," not in the sense of abandoning self-discipline, but in the sense of learning we're not God and learning to entrust ourselves to the one on heaven's throne.

"Hallowed be Your Name"

The first petition gives us an important glimpse into what ultimately matters: "Hallowed be your name." This petition concerns both the church's worship and her mission. We pray, in essence, "May we honor your name and worship you as is fitting to your glory," and, "May the world see your goodness and offer you the reverence due your name." The church's worship and her mission are integrally related. As my friend Mark Young puts it, "We will not commend to the world a God we do not adore." This prayer commits us to worship and mission. We cannot pray for God's name to be hallowed in our lives and in the world and not be willing to live in such a way that would bring about that end. For God to grant this petition would be for him to bless the church and her mission so deeply that the world would see and honor him.

And that inevitability leads to the recognition of our failure to live this prayer faithfully, to consistently live lives that hallow God's name. One of the most profound books I've read on the Lord's Prayer is Helmut Thielicke's *The Prayer That Spans the World*. The power of the book comes not only from Thielicke's tremendous insight and graceful articulation, but also from knowing that his words were originally delivered as sermons to the faithful community of Christians in Stuttgart who continued to gather around the gospel of grace and the table of the Eucharist throughout the horrors of the air raids, the final days of Hitler's reign of terror, and the chaos and uncertainty of the beginning of the period of occupation. Against that backdrop Thielicke writes, "The truth is that we cannot pray the Lord's Prayer to the glory of God unless at the same time we pray it against ourselves. And he who has not yet learned to pray this prayer *de profundis*, out of the depths of repentance, has not really learned to pray at all."[21] To pray "Hallowed be thy name" is to admit that God's name often plays all too small a part in our everyday lives. But, Thielicke notes, there is no petition in the prayer that says, "Lord lead me to further sanctification in my life." That is not to say that such prayers are illegitimate, but to simply observe that in the pattern prayer that Jesus gives us, he "turns our attention away from ourselves, even from our pious selves, and concentrates it upon the Father. The prayer is not 'May I be hallowed' but 'thy name be hallowed.'"[22] To pray this petition is to pray for God to do his work in us, turning us out from ourselves and toward his glory and the good of our neighbors.

"Your Kingdom Come"

Jesus insisted that in his life and ministry the kingdom of God had come (see Mark 1:15), yet he still taught his disciples to plead with God that the kingdom would yet come. As Frederick Buechner has observed,

> Insofar as here and there, and now and then, God's kingly will is being done in various odd ways among us even at this moment, the kingdom has come already. Insofar as all the odd ways we do his will at this moment are at best half-baked and half-hearted, the kingdom is still a long way off—a hell of a long way off, to be more precise and theological.[23]

In the incarnate life, ignominious death and victorious resurrection of Jesus, the world decisively turned a corner from darkness to light, from death to life, from the dominion of sin and the devil to the reign of God. And yet we still find ourselves surrounded by brokenness at every turn. The answer to Paul's question "Where, O death, is your sting?" (1 Corinthians 15:55) is obvious. It's all around us. Sin, death and the devil still seem to hold sway.

This petition of the Lord's Prayer is the prayer par excellence of the vision of God. It is a prayer that God's kingdom would come here and come now to set the world right. It is a prayer for God's personal presence, God's just reign and God's perfect peace. In praying this prayer we are pledging our allegiance to this coming kingdom and relinquishing our allegiance to kingdoms of this world.

Often we are accustomed to praying to God for what we want. We make our requests with fingers crossed, hoping God will give us what we've asked for. But in praying the way Jesus taught us—both in this prayer and in Gethsemane—we are "attempting to school ourselves to want what God wants."[24] "Not my will, but yours be done" (Luke 22:42). To pray, "Your will be done" is not a prayer of resignation, a shrug of the shoulders that says, "What I want doesn't really matter." It is to pray that what's wrong would be made right, what's broken would be made whole, what's marred would be made beautiful. Praying this prayer with regularity trains us to long for that to be realized, to crave it with an increasing intensity and to allow that yearning to put all other desires and requests into a much larger perspective. It teaches us to cherish God's will more and more and our own will less and less.

"Our Daily Bread"

Human beings may not live by bread alone, but we definitely can't live without it. In this petition Jesus teaches us to pray for our most basic needs. For some the prayer for daily bread is a desperate plea that names what they need most, the simple provision of "enough for today." But for most who will read this book, the problem is that we have more than we need. How can we meaningfully pray for bread for the day when we've got well-stocked cupboards? For one, this prayer reminds us that despite all appearances to the contrary, we are fragile, dependent creatures. We live in a society that disdains the notion of dependence. But praying as Jesus taught us is a way to be reminded that all we have ultimately comes to us from the hand of God.

Second, praying for our daily bread is a helpful reminder that no bread is ours alone. Our dependence for today's bread is not only on God but also on the farmers, the bakers, the delivery drivers, the grocers—and the list goes on. By the time it arrives at our tables it has passed through many hands. It has come to us through the hard work, sacrifice and gifts of strangers. We do well to pay attention to how it has come to our table and to cultivate a sense of gratitude by becoming more aware of those who have contributed to its production.

Finally, this prayer ought to awaken us to an awareness of those with and for whom we pray who don't have pantries full of bread for today and plenty left for tomorrow. Throughout their history, those who have prayed this prayer have felt a burden to share their bread with the hungry.

The bread for which we pray is *our* bread. If we pray this prayer in earnest, we should be willing to allow God to use us in his answer to our request. To pray for our daily bread obligates us. The fourth-century Christian leader Basil the Great put the matter this way: "The bread that you possess belongs to the hungry. The clothes that you store in boxes, belong to the naked. The shoes rotting by you, belong to the bare-foot. The money that you hide belongs to anyone in need."[25] What if God has given some of us more than we need not merely as a "blessing" to be hoarded, but as a means of answering the prayer of those who pray for daily bread—that through the ones who have plenty God might provide for the ones who are in need? This is what we hold in mind when we pray for "our daily bread."

"Forgive Us . . . As We Forgive"

To pray as Jesus taught us is to pray for the restoration of shalom, and to take that seriously inevitably brings us face to face with the problem of sin in our lives and in the world. Early on in this book I introduced the understanding of sin as "the vandalism of shalom" and suggested that we all experience the vandalism of shalom because of our own foolish, sinful choices, because of the harm done to us by others over which we have no control, and because of the reality of living in a fallen world filled with suffering and death. To pray, "Forgive us our debts, as we also have forgiven our debtors" touches on each of these aspects of the vandalism of shalom. Each of us has been wrapped up in the tendrils of the world, the flesh and the devil. Before we consider the gravity of the wrongs we have suffered at the hands of others, we must ponder the gravity of what God has suffered by our own hands. The Book of Common Prayer includes the following daily confession:

> Most merciful God,
> we confess that we have sinned against you
> in thought, word, and deed,
> by what we have done,
> and by what we have left undone.
> We have not loved you with our whole heart;
> we have not loved our neighbors as ourselves.
> We are truly sorry and we humbly repent.

For the sake of your Son Jesus Christ,
have mercy on us and forgive us;
that we may delight in your will,
and walk in your ways,
to the glory of your Name. Amen.

Such a prayer can become a powerful means of daily self-examination as we consider before God how its expression of both confession and repentance reflect the reality of our hearts and lives. All that this prayer says is bound up in the words "forgive us our debts."

But Jesus calls us in this prayer to acknowledge and live in light of the reality that if we have been forgiven, we must also be forgivers. To fail to do so is, in an important sense, to cut off the branch on which we're sitting. In calling us to forgive, Jesus is not condoning or belittling the injustice we have suffered. God takes sin seriously. We need look no further than the cross to see that. But when we look to the cross we see the seriousness of our own sin. As Bonhoeffer has said, for the one who looks to the cross, the "spirit of judgment is cut off at the roots. He knows the other to be accepted by God in the midst of his lostness even as he is accepted."[26] To pray this way is to acknowledge that the debts of our offenders are infinitely less than our own debt before God and that we all stand on level ground at the foot of the cross. Learning to forgive as we are forgiven can be a painful process. But it is fundamental to praying as Jesus taught us.

Finally, when we pray this prayer in solidarity with the world that doesn't know the one to whom we pray, we pray for the forgiving love of God to reach those who are far from him. When we pray this prayer we must lift our eyes from ourselves and see the sin and brokenness of the world. Where do we see the world groaning under the weight of the vandalism of shalom, longing for the fullness of redemption? Where are God's image bearers being neglected, exploited, brutalized or oppressed? Where are they blinded by political or religious ideology that keeps them unaware or ill-informed of the God who loves them? Where do disease, decay and death appear triumphant? All of these we hold in our hands and lift to our Father when we pray, "Forgive us."

"Deliver Us from Evil"

To pray, "Lead us not into temptation, but deliver us from the evil one," is to acknowledge the reality and gravity of evil in the world. We inhabit a world locked in conflict between a kingdom in decline—the dominion of sin, death and the devil—and a kingdom on the rise—the coming reign of justice and peace. The world, the flesh and the devil—the enemies of the soul—conspire against God and therefore against us. To pray the words that Jesus taught us is to recognize that evil continues to wield its destructive power but also to declare our confidence in the victory of Jesus. Jesus' words here are not an indication that God himself tempts us. They are rather a plea that God would preserve us from temptation and testing beyond our ability to bear and enable us to pass through a world that is still "not the way it's supposed to be" without being so overwhelmed that we lose sight of the dream of God for a world set right. To pray this way is to acknowledge that we are not the masters of our own fate, that our ability to withstand the way things are and live in light of the way things ought to be rests on a power beyond us. Here we acknowledge that God himself is greater than any rival, that evil is strong but God is stronger, and that we desperately need his power to save and to deliver.

Praying the Vision in Everyday Life

As I mentioned above, one early Christian discipleship manual instructed followers of Jesus to pray the Lord's Prayer three times a day, every single day. This rhythm of prayer at appointed times woven throughout the day was part of the early church's inheritance from Judaism. Jesus and his earliest followers were formed in a Jewish culture shaped by this "three-times-a-day-we-all-stop-and-pray-together sacred rhythm."[27] This way of marking time cultivated in them a sense of attentiveness and receptivity to God that permeated the remainder of the day. In the busy, distracted world we live in, we would do well to recover this early Christian pattern of prayer at set times interlaced throughout the day. Adopting a rhythm of praying the prayer Jesus taught us, or using this prayer as our model, allows us to be immersed in a long tradition and vocabulary of prayer that is permeated with the vision of God. It also connects us in a bond of unity with other Christians who pray this prayer in different time zones and languages every day all over the world. Adopting such a rhythm also can sustain us in the practice of prayer in times of spiritual dryness.

In prayer we pay attention to God. In prayer we open ourselves to his work. In prayer our lives are turned outward from ourselves and toward God's name, God's kingdom, God's world. In praying the prayer that Jesus taught us, we find our voices and our lives swept up into the drama of what God is doing to rescue and renew his good but broken creation. This is a prayer of breathing in and breathing out, a prayer of spirituality and mission. To pray this prayer is to commit ourselves to be used by God as a small part of the way he answers this prayer in the world. And we reinforce this commitment every time we say "amen." Most Christians have become so accustomed to saying "amen" at the end of our prayers that it has become for many of us little more than an empty cipher that signals to God and everybody else, "We're done now." But the Greek word *amen* would have carried with it the force of "let it be." We conclude our prayers with one final plea: "So be it!" Packed into that one little word, so often overlooked, is a plea to God to accomplish all we have asked through the redeeming work of Christ and the active agency of the Holy Spirit in the world, and to let it begin with us.

The Work of the People

Practicing the Vision in Corporate Worship

Worship names what matters most:
the way human beings are created to reflect
God's glory by embodying God's character in lives that seek
righteousness and do justice. . . . Worship turns out to be the dangerous
act of waking up to God and to the purposes of God in the world,
and then living lives that actually show it.

MARK LABBERTON

Worship does God's story.

ROBERT WEBBER

On a sweltering summer day just over a decade ago, I found myself sitting alone next to an open window on a bus heading to the outskirts of Rome. Three weeks earlier my wife and I had flown across the Atlantic to spend a month in Europe. The plan was for us to spend nineteen days in Spain serving in a variety of ministry capacities and then for the two of us to spend ten days in Italy taking in the beauty, culture and history of the country.

There was only one complication to our plans. Just before we were to leave, my wife found out she was pregnant with our first child. We weighed the decision to go for several days, but in light of the fact that she hadn't felt the slightest tinge of morning sickness, we decided to venture out.

Everything was fine until we got about half way across the ocean, at which point she became miserably sick, a condition that hardly improved for the remainder of the trip. That's how I found myself alone on the bus that afternoon. On our last full day in Rome, she couldn't even bring herself to leave the hotel room. But she insisted that I go take in one of the sites that I desperately wanted to see while we were there, the ancient Roman catacombs.

I managed to find my way onto a bus that would take me out through the crumbling ancient city walls and along the historic Via Appia to the Catacombs of Saint Domitilla. When I arrived at the site, I paid my admission and descended a long flight of stone stairs that led into a series of cold, dark underground caves—eleven miles of crisscrossing tunnels that date back to the earliest days of Christian history. Our group, led by a young British woman, walked down the dimly lit corridor where every few feet, on my right and on my left, there was a place carved out in the rock to lay a body. These tunnels were dug as burial places for Christians who died in the first few centuries of the church, many of whom died a martyr's death.

We entered into one hallway where the lights, perhaps all too conveniently, had gone out. Our group gathered as close as we could to the flickering flame of the tour guide's cigarette lighter. In that moment I could not help but think about the early Christians who had gathered in those caves by the dim light of a tiny oil lamp to worship together— safe, at least for the moment, from the threat of persecution. They gathered in that very place, surrounded by the corpses of their fallen sisters and brothers, to share the bread and wine of the Eucharist, to sing and pray, and to honor the martyrs.

For many in my group I think those dank caves represented little more than a curiosity of history. But for me the space was sacred. As I stood there amid the tombs of those nameless heroes, I remember being profoundly struck by two things about them: the depth of their spiritual experience and the breadth of their missional impact.

In the midst of an intensely inhospitable cultural environment, the Christians of the earliest centuries of the church demonstrated a radical commitment to the way of Jesus. Jesus had called his followers to "take up their cross and follow," and many early Christians died fulfilling that call. But despite the many cultural disincentives, the gospel message spread like wildfire and the church grew rapidly throughout the Roman Empire. Those early Christians became known for their demonstrable love toward neighbors and enemies, and their embodied witness to the truth they had encountered in Christ made an immense impact on the world around them. In one of the periods of history when the church's relationship to the surrounding cultural environment was at its most hostile, the church grew by a remarkable rate of approximately forty percent per decade.[1] According to one Christian apologist writing around the year 200, "Beauty of life causes strangers to join the ranks. . . . We do not preach great things; we live them."[2] Theirs was a life with God for the world. And the world noticed.

In an essay on the missional character of the earliest generations of Christians, historian Alan Kreider paints a compelling picture of the "beauty of life" the Christian communities embodied that made them so attractive to their non-Christian neighbors. But, importantly, Kreider goes beyond describing their form of life to ask the question, "How did they become that kind of people?" How did they come to live such beautiful lives in front of their neighbors? One of the central features Kreider points to is the Christians' practice of gathering for corporate worship. He writes, "The church's evangelism and mission were inconceivable without the church's life of worship. The church assembled in worship glorified God; their actions of worship also edified Christians who, formed by worship, lived the question posing life of God in the world."[3]

Since I teach graduate courses in the area of spiritual formation, I am asked from time to time to consult with local church leaders interested in leading their congregations into a greater emphasis on spiritual formation. They are usually slightly taken aback when one of the first things I suggest is that if their church wants to take spiritual formation seriously then they need to take seriously what they say and do in the context of corporate worship. The common assumption of many of these church leaders is that to engage in spiritual formation at a congregational level will mean the development of some new program or the reconfiguring of existing programs for different purposes. They are not helped along by much of the contemporary literature on spiritual formation, which often makes corporate worship at best a supplement and at worst completely superfluous and subordinate to private individual practices. But throughout the church's history, one of the primary means of pursuing spiritual formation has been immersion in the liturgical rhythms of the church's life together. Debra Rienstra calls the community gathered for worship "the central workshop where God engages in his soul-shaping work."[4]

The word *liturgy* no doubt makes some folks nervous, conjuring up thoughts of "smells and bells," the recitation of rote prayers and the performance of empty rituals.[5] But etymologically the word simply means "the work of the people." Liturgy refers to what the people of God do when they gather to present themselves before him for worship, prayer and instruction. In this most basic understanding of the term, even the most free-spirited "contemporary" churches have a liturgy. My use of the terminology of "liturgy" and "liturgical" in this chapter will employ this more general usage. My focus will be on the need for churches to think carefully about the role of liturgy in the cultivation of the kind of spirituality being advocated throughout this book. My concern is more with function than with form. But as will become clear, the distinction between form and function is not nearly as neat and clean as some might prefer. In other words, it may be that in order to recover the function embedded in the ancient liturgical rhythms I'll be considering below, we need to take seriously the forms in which they were embedded. What I am ultimately advocating is the creative, contextualized recovery of these ancient liturgical rhythms for the cultivation of life with God for the world.

The Formative Power of Worship

Before proceeding to discuss the formative power of corporate worship, I need to make a few important caveats. The first is simply to point out that worship ought not be construed primarily in terms of what it accomplishes. William Willimon suggests that the greatest temptation in American Christian worship is utilitarianism, thinking of worship primarily in terms of its usefulness. He writes, "Worship loses its integrity when it is regarded instrumentally as a means to something else—even as a means of achieving the most noble of human purposes, even the noble purpose of moral edification."[6] Worship is first and foremost about God, about gathering to offer him the praise he is due. God doesn't need our worship, but he deserves it and delights in it. The formative significance of worship comes, as it were, as a byproduct of our pursuit of its primary purpose. As we gather to worship God we are being transformed into his image. As Debra Dean Murphy has put it, "The destination and the means are the same: the praise and adoration of God."[7]

A second important caveat is that the worship gathering is not the sole or even the primary expression of what it means to be the church. In the minds of many, all talk of church calls to mind the image of the Sunday gathering. We "go to church," meaning we show up to a common place at a common time for our common experience of worship. But as Michael Frost points out, "The idea of worshiping with fellow believers and then bidding them farewell in the parking lot—'See you next Sunday'—is the very antithesis of the experience of the earliest Christians."[8] For the early Christians, the fullness of their experience of church could be captured by three Greek words: *leitourgia, koinonia* and *diakonia. Leitourgia*—the "work of the people"—referred to their gathering for public worship. But this gathering was deeply interwoven with and dependent on their *koinonia,* their common life together. *Koinonia* is often translated by the word "fellowship," but that is too thin a word for many of us (especially those with memories of bad potluck dinners in the fellowship hall). *Koinonia* is a rich word that refers to shared life lived in intimate community. It is sharing one another's joys and burdens. It is walking together in the details of daily life. Apart from a deep experience of *koinonia,* our corporate worship gathering too easily devolves into a kind of individual spectator experience that we all happen to have in the same time and place week after week. *Leitourgia* and *koinonia* go hand in hand.

And our *leitourgia* and *koinonia* are (or ought to be) inextricably bound up with our *diakonia*—our "service" or "ministry." Sadly, far too many Christians have come to believe that there are two kinds of Christians in the church: the professionals who do ministry and the rest of us to whom ministry is done. But in Ephesians 4, Paul makes it explicitly clear that God has gifted some members of the community with specific gifts to equip the entire community "for the work of ministry"—for *diakonia* (Ephesians 4:11). *Diakonia* is the calling of the entire community to participate in the mission of God in the world. It is our collective vocation to give ourselves away in service for the glory of God and the good of other people. And no one is exempt. Every Christian is "called to ministry." Our "breathing in" in worship comes both as response to and preparation for our "breathing out" in mission.

A third caveat that needs to be made about worship is the honest acknowledgment that many of our mainstream experiences of worship don't actually form us in the ways I am spelling out in this chapter. Week in and week out, worshipers emerge from thousands of church gatherings to live lives that are barely distinguishable from those of the surrounding culture. I believe that this is often the result of either an unreflective traditionalism or an unreflective consumerism on the part of both those who design worship experiences and the worshipers themselves.

On the one hand, our worship gatherings can be designed and engaged in a way that amounts to simply going through the motions. Little thought is given on the part of the leaders or the participants to the formative dimension of what we are doing. Instead we follow the established patterns. We employ whatever template we have received from the tradition of which we are a part. Scant attention is given to creativity, contextualization or the form of life our liturgies are intended to promote.

On the other hand, many contemporary worship experiences that do take creativity and context seriously do so not for the purpose of forming a people for the mission of God but for attracting people to attend their church. Enormous amounts of time, energy and money are spent on the weekly gathering, producing services that are culturally savvy, emotionally engaging and relevant to daily life. None of those descriptors inherently compromise the integrity of our worship. The problem comes when those things take center stage in a way that reduces the worship gathering to a marketing device crafted to appeal to savvy religious consumers. Then the criteria for evaluation of our worship becomes the post-service buzz and the number of return attendees rather than whether or not our congregation is faithfully pursuing the mission of God during the other six days of the week.

God intends to form us as his missional people when we gather to worship him. There are four ways that corporate worship nurtures and sustains our life with God for the world: worship redefines our identity, worship reorders our affections, worship repatterns our imagination, and worship reorients our life in the world.

First, worship redefines our identity. According to the Eastern Orthodox theologian Alexander Schmemann, to be human is to be *homo adorans*, the being that worships.[9] We are made to worship and, in fact, cannot *not* worship. The issue is not whether we will worship but what we will worship. The problem of sin is fundamentally a problem of misplaced worship, elevating something, someone or some act to a higher place of adoration and trust in our heart than God. This problem is exacerbated by a cultural environment that shapes us to be not *homo adorans* but *homo consumens*[10]—not the being that worships but the being that consumes, not the being that gives the gift of adoration but the being that takes what he or she can get. As Debra Dean Murray points out, our North American cultural environment is deeply marked by "a complex, systematic web of practices and beliefs through which persons are socialized from a very early age to expect the immediate satisfaction of all desire—physical and emotional, material and psychological."[11] Sadly, the effects of this culturally mediated notion of human identity have even crept into and transformed some Christian worship practices. Murphy asks pointedly,

> How do we reckon with the truth that we in the church have become, for all intents and purposes, a society of strangers? That we enter into worship bringing a numbing passivity born of media bombardment and image overkill, a self-preoccupation created and nurtured by an increasingly therapeutic, individualistic, and narcissistic culture, and the not-so-tacit assumption that worship is but another attractively packaged commodity to be consumed by a savvy, discriminating, church-shopping public?[12]

This way of construing the corporate worship gathering produces in us precisely the opposite of worship's intended effect. Gathering for worship ought to entail our being reminded who we're made to be, being reminded that we are most human when we worship the one who created and sustains us out of his inexhaustible grace.

But to be reminded that human beings are created to worship God also involves being reminded that proper worship entails a certain kind of life. Our identity entails a vocation, a calling, to represent the reign of God. To be made in the image of God is not so much a property of our humanity as it is a task, a mission. Our true worship is to offer our whole self as a "living sacrifice" in fulfilling this vocation. We gather to be reminded of our identity and vocation. We are sent to live it out.

Second, worship reorders our affections. The idea that corporate worship reorders our affections is closely connected to the notion that we are fundamentally beings who worship. We worship that which we love the most. The public worship gathering is a school for our affections, a space in our lives where we take our eyes off the things we love more than we ought and put them, as it were, on the one we ought to love more than we do.

To worship is to acknowledge and honor the worth of God. In worship we put the love of God on display so we can be reminded of why he is worthy of our worship. Thus, the gospel ought to be at the center of all Christian worship: "This is love: not that we loved God, but that he loved us and sent his Son as an atoning sacrifice for our sins" (1 John 4:10). When we truly encounter the depth of God's love for us and all creation, it naturally evokes a response of worship.

When I was a kid we used to sing a song with a line that said, "Nothing I desire compares with you." It was a song that, quite frankly, got a little tired after a while because we sang it a lot and always sang the same little chorus over and over. Usually when we sang it, my head and my heart checked out. But then one night it occurred to me that I was lying to God. Certainly it's true to say that nothing I desire compares with him in terms of its being worthy of my love and allegiance. But both then and now there are things in my life that compete with him for my love and allegiance. We gather for public worship to be reminded of the reality that nothing we desire truly compares with him and to have our affections retuned to their proper order.

Third, worship repatterns our imagination. Walter Brueggemann has suggested that corporate worship entails "a subversive re-imagining of reality."[13] As we rehearse God's story in worship—through song, sacrament, prayer and sermon—we are reminded of the way things were in creation and the way things will be when the dream of God is fully realized and God sets the world right. This looking back and looking ahead—the two fundamental movements in the worship of both Israel and the church—shapes the way we see and engage the world as we live suspended between what God has done and what God will do. In looking back and looking ahead we are poignantly reminded that the world as we know it is "not the way it's supposed to be."

We cannot embody a form of life that we can't first imagine. Corporate worship is the place where the vision of God—the vision of God's personal presence, God's just reign and God's perfect peace—seizes our imagination as we gather to sing songs and tell stories that put that vision on display. Worship that repatterns our imagination draws us into the dream of God for a world set right and, over time, helps us conceive ways to arrange our lives differently to live in anticipation of God's dream coming to fruition.

Perhaps one of the most profound ways to illustrate how worship repatterns Christian imagination is to point back to the place of the church and its worship in the lives of the heroes of the civil rights movement. They sang songs that promised "we shall overcome" and they heard rousing sermons that pointed ahead to a day when "justice will roll down like water and righteousness like an ever-flowing stream." Their worship enabled them to imagine the world differently than so many of them experienced in the Jim Crow South. And having their imagination captivated by a vision of a different world generated the moral courage within to work for a world that looked more like they imagined, even if that meant their own profound sacrifice and suffering to see that world realized. Where did they find the fortitude to defiantly but nonviolently resist the fire hoses, the police dogs, the baseball bats and the burning crosses? They found it in worship.

To have hope is to believe tenaciously in a world that doesn't exist yet. But when that hope really gets down deep in our bones, it changes the way we live in the world as we know it. We do not meet the world as it is with a pessimistic surrender but with a defiant resolve to fashion foretastes of an as-yet-unrealized future. And that kind of hope is nurtured and sustained when the church gathers for worship.

Finally, worship reorients our life in the world. The test of authentic worship is whether lives are transformed and living out the mission of God. As Richard Foster has said, "If worship does not propel us to greater obedience, it has not been worship."[14] Worship ushers us into the transforming presence of God. There our identity is redefined, our affections are reordered and our imaginations are repatterned. But the only way to determine whether any of this has genuinely taken place is to look at the lives of the worshipers during the rest of the week. Our faithful attendance and passionate expression in corporate worship is meaningless—in fact, abhorrent to God—if not accompanied by a commitment to love and serve people who are broken and in need. Genuine worship compels us to concrete acts of justice, tangible demonstrations of compassion and embodied expressions of the love and grace of God directed toward those who are far from him.

One great threat to authentic Christian worship that many congregations face in North America today is that our gatherings become therapeutic rather than transformative. It's far easier to sing songs, pray prayers and preach sermons that help us feel better about ourselves and the world than to sing songs, pray prayers and preach sermons that call for deep change in us so that we might become agents of deep change in the world. And the former will fill a large auditorium much more quickly than the latter. While it is certainly not inappropriate to celebrate the great love God has lavished on us or to praise him for the comfort his presence provides, when the center of gravity in our worship shifts from the greatness of God and his glorious mission to rescue and renew the lost and broken to the benefits we enjoy that flow from him, our worship becomes more an exercise in self-affirmation, more a means of coping with the status quo, than a means of reorienting our life in the world. Corporate worship is not supposed to be food for the ego but fuel for the mission. It is not supposed to reinforce the inward turn of the soul but is to be one of the primary means by which we are turned upward toward God and then outward toward our neighbors.

There is an ancient Latin maxim that has long guided the church's thinking about worship: *lex orandi, lex credendi*—"the law of prayer is the law of belief." A helpful paraphrase would be "As the church prays [or worships], so she believes." This understanding guided theological expression in the early church as its thinkers began to formulate doctrine that accurately reflected what it affirmed about the Father, Son and Spirit in prayer and liturgy. It continues to function today, for example, in the way that many of us first learn that God is triune—not through some formal theological instruction but through singing "Holy, holy, holy, Lord God Almighty, God in three persons, blessed Trinity." As the church worships, so she believes. But sometimes this formulation is helpfully expanded to include a third movement: *lex orandi, lex credendi, lex vivendi*—"as the church worships, so she believes, so she lives." What we say to and about God in the context of corporate worship ought to deeply shape what we believe is true about him, about ourselves and about the world. And that belief ought to visibly work its way into the pattern of life we embody in our day-to-day reality. Worship that doesn't lead us to give our lives away for the glory of God and the good of other people hasn't been true worship.

Liturgical Rhythms

Having considered what worship does—its formative significance—we now turn our attention to how worship does it. What are the liturgical rhythms that, week in and week out, nurture and sustain life with God for the world? There are five of these rhythms that have historically characterized Christian worship gatherings.

Confessing our sin. While it has become less and less common in many contemporary expressions of worship, the public confession of sin has long stood as one of the nonnegotiable elements of Christian liturgy. And that makes a lot of sense. If part of what it means to gather for worship is to be ushered collectively into the presence of God, the natural response to recognition of his presence is a corresponding recognition of our own unworthiness to be there. This was true of Isaiah the prophet, who, after encountering the presence of the Lord in his temple, declared, "Woe to me! . . . I am ruined! For I am a man of unclean lips, and I live among a people of unclean lips" (Isaiah 6:5). It was also true for Peter, the fisherman, who after recognizing the holiness of the one who had climbed in his boat threw himself at the feet of Jesus and cried, "Go away from me, Lord; I am a sinful man!" (Luke 5:8).

In public confession we name the reality that the world is not the way it's supposed to be and that each of us is in some way complicit in that reality. It is to acknowledge, as the Book of Common Prayer puts it, that "we have followed too much the devices and desires of our own hearts. . . . We have left undone those things which we ought to have done; and we have done those things which we ought not to have done." As James K. A. Smith has said, "The very reason that we are gathered for worship under the cross is because of humanity's fundamental failure to carry out the task and mission of being the image of God."[15] We have failed in our human vocation to ensure that God's will is done on earth as it is in heaven, and each of us—in big ways and small ways—persists in that failure. The logic of the liturgy is that it is best to acknowledge that reality before God and one another rather than to ignore it, hide it or pretend it isn't true. Bonhoeffer reminds us that, in confession, "you don't have to go on lying to yourself and to other

Christians as if you were without sin. You are allowed to be a sinner."[16]

But in our corporate act of confession we not only acknowledge the truth of our sin; we plead with God to accomplish his restorative intention in our lives. One Presbyterian prayer of confession ends with the lines, "Lord, have mercy upon us; heal us and forgive us. Set us free to serve you in the world as agents of your reconciling love in Jesus Christ. Amen."[17] The point of confession is not to wallow in our guilt but to experience the restoration and renewal we need.

In this act of truth-telling we open ourselves to the power of the gospel and are reminded again of our vocation. Those traditional liturgies that involve public confession also involve the declaration of pardon. According to Clayton Schmidt, "The pronouncement of absolution or pardon always follows corporate confession. If there is any inviolable liturgical rule, this is it. . . . Words of absolution are among the most powerful and meaningful spoken in worship."[18] Here we hear the words of promise: "If we confess our sins, he is faithful and just and will forgive us our sins and purify us from all unrighteousness" (1 John 1:9). We are assured that "there is now no condemnation for those who are in Christ Jesus, because through Christ Jesus the law of the Spirit who gives life has set you free from the law of sin and death" (Romans 8:1-2). In the confession of sin and the declaration of pardon we are profoundly reminded, as James K. A. Smith puts it, "A reordering of creation has already broken into creation in the person of Jesus Christ, and we are gathering as a people in order to practice for the arrival of the kingdom in its fullness—and thus in order to be trained to be a kingdom-kind-of-people in the meantime, as witnesses to that kingdom, in and through our work as cultural agents."[19]

Rehearsing our story. When the gathered church sings songs, recites creeds and reads Scripture, we are rehearsing the story of God. One of the most frequently voiced commands throughout the Scripture is the command "sing." Singing is a practice that engages our bodies, our affections and our imaginations simultaneously in powerful ways. Songs have a way of getting down in our bones in ways that other forms of communication simply can't. Songs have a unique capacity to inform our minds, to stir our souls and to engender hope.

In light of the formative potential of the songs we sing, it seems to me that we need better songs. We need songs that aren't burdened by sappy sentimentalism—songs of the "Jesus is my boyfriend" variety. It isn't at all inappropriate to sing of God's great love for us or of our corresponding love for him. But many of today's worship songs trivialize that love relationship by attempting to capture it in a romantic (even erotic) idiom. We need songs that celebrate the sent and sending God who is pursuing his dream of a world set right, songs that describe that world, that celebrate what God has done though Christ to make that world a reality, and that call us to our role as signs and foretastes of that world. We need songs of remembrance and revolution.

Perhaps the most important word in the worship of the people of ancient Israel was the Hebrew word *zakar*—remember. Israel's worship was predicated on remembering what God had done, his mighty deeds of deliverance, his faithfulness in preserving his people. In Psalm 77:11-12, the psalmist writes,

I will remember the deeds of the LORD;
    yes, I will remember your miracles of long ago.
I will consider all your works
    and meditate on all your mighty deeds.

The psalm goes on to rehearse the history of God's mighty acts of deliverance of his people in the exodus and his appearance to them at Sinai. Israel sang songs of remembrance in order that they might be sustained in hope no matter their circumstances. The God who has acted in the past is capable of acting in the present and will act again in the future.

Christian worship has long been characterized by the same look back to God's mighty deeds, most profoundly expressed in the passion and resurrection of Jesus. In the late second century, Melito of Sardis wrote,

> When the Lord had clothed himself with humanity,
> and had suffered for the sake of the sufferer,
> and had been bound for the sake of the imprisoned,
> and had been judged for the sake of the condemned,
> and was buried for the sake of the one who was buried,
> he rose up from the dead,
> and cried with a loud voice:
> Who is he that contends with me?
> Let him stand in opposition to me.
> I set the condemned man free;
> I gave the dead man life;
> I raised up one who had been entombed.
> Who is my opponent?
> I, he says, am the Christ.
> I am the one who destroyed death,
> and triumphed over the enemy,
> and trampled Hades underfoot,
> and bound the strong one,
> and carried off man to the heights of heaven,
> I, he says, am the Christ.

Melito's great hymn of the triumphant Christ sustained Christians suffering under the weight of imperial oppression by calling them to remember the victory of the one they were called to follow. The church today needs powerful songs of remembrance that can give us courage and strength as we seek to follow Jesus in our own unique cultural time and place.

But in addition to songs of remembrance, we need songs of revolution. According to Jacques Ellul, "If the Christian is not being revolutionary, then in some way or another he has been unfaithful to his calling in the world."[20] To be revolutionary, according to Ellul, means "bringing the future into the present as an explosive force. It means believing that future events are more important and more true than present events; it means understanding the present in light of the future."[21] He goes on,

> The Christian is essentially a person who lives in expectation. This expectation is directed toward the return of the Lord which accompanies the end of time, the Judgment, and proclaims the Kingdom of God. . . . [The Christian] looks forward to this moment, and for him all facts acquire their value in the light of the coming of the Kingdom of God, in the light of the Judgment, and the victory of God.

If Christians today are to live in such a way as to bring "the future into the present as an explosive force," we need songs that help us imagine that future, that stir our affections for that future, that nurture in us a deep desire to see that future arrive.

Hearing God's Word. In one of the oldest descriptions of Christian worship outside of the New Testament, Justin Martyr writes, "And on the day called Sunday, all who live in cities or in the country gather together to one place, and the memoirs of the apostles or the writings of the prophets are read, as long as time permits; then, when the reader has ceased, the president verbally instructs, and exhorts to the imitation of these good things."[22] As Justin's words make clear, from the earliest days of the church, Christians have been "people of the book" and the Scriptures have held a place of prominence in their worship. Traditionally, there has been a considerable amount of time and attention given in the worship gathering to the reading and preaching of the Bible.

Walter Brueggemann suggests that the "primal task" of the one who stands to preach is "the narration and nurture of a counter-identity."[23] He writes, "The preacher is not called upon to do all the parts of public policy and public morality, but to give spine, resolve, courage, energy, and freedom that belong to a counteridentity."[24] Brueggemann draws parallels between the condition of the church in North America today and the condition of Israel in exile, and he suggests that the preacher's task is to help the church resist the forces of our Babylon that would seek to press us into its mold. Sadly, the most esteemed preachers of our day are often not the ones preaching such provocative, countercultural sermons but those who have mastered the art of making Christianity palatable to savvy religious consumers. Kierkegaard's description of the popular preacher of his day sounds very much like today's skilled orator schooled by the best of the church growth literature:

> A nimble, adroit man, who in pretty language, with the utmost ease, with graceful manners . . . knows how to introduce a little Christianity, but easily, as easily as possible. In the New Testament, Christianity is the profoundest wound that can be inflicted upon a man, calculated on the most dreadful scale to collide with everything—and now the clergyman has perfected himself in introducing Christianity in such a$ way as it signifies nothing, and when he is able to do this to perfection he is regarded as a paragon. But this is nauseating![25]

The Bible has the capacity to both comfort the afflicted and afflict the comfortable. It isn't out to flatter us but to transform us. It isn't primarily interested in making sense of our lives as they already are but in dismantling and remaking us. As N. T. Wright has said, "The Bible is breathed out by God . . . so that it can fashion and form God's people to do his work in the world."[26] This happens as the preacher, week after week, sermon after sermon, in a thousand different ways, echoes the words of Jesus to the congregation, "Repent and believe the gospel."

Frederick Buechner suggests that sermons are a lot like jokes. Even the best ones are hard to remember.[27] Thankfully, the point of listening to sermons is not so much to remember them but to submit oneself to their cumulative effect, so that over time they come to shape a consciousness and a way of life.

Sharing God's table. Having rehearsed the story of God in our worship—looking back and looking ahead—we enact that story when we come to the table of the Lord's Supper. Seeing the formative power of coming to the table rests on four simple but important observations. First, we sometimes call it "Communion" because it celebrates our union with God made available through Jesus' sacrifice on the cross. As such it is a meal of compassion, acceptance and forgiveness. We who were God's enemies have become his friends through the reconciling work of Jesus. "He himself is our peace" (Ephesians 2:14). He now invites us into this profound act of welcome, the fellowship of his table. We become people whose lives are increasingly marked by hospitality when we contemplate the hospitality of God expressed at this table.

Second, in calling it "Communion" we're also reminded that this act both symbolizes and makes real our union with other believers who share in the hope we have though Christ. As William Willimon writes, "The Lord's Supper, Communion, has much to do with the expression and the formation of community. In our present hunger for community, we should never forget that the central, historic, constitutive, communal act of the church has been its celebrations of the Lord's Supper."[28] The prayer of Jesus for his church was that we would be one. Our unity is predicated on the grace of God in Christ. The peace he has won for us is not only peace with God; it is peace with each other. Every time we receive the elements we're called to reconciliation.

Third, we sometimes call this act "the Eucharist," an ancient name that comes from the Greek word for giving thanks. We come to the table out of gratitude to God for what Christ has done for us. And our participation nurtures that gratitude in us. Too often we approach the Eucharist with great solemnity, as though it were an act of mourning. It is, in fact, an act of joy. And it is a reminder that we are meant to live eucharistic lives, lives deeply marked by gratitude and therefore offered back to God as an expression of worship. Our regular participation in the Eucharist is a recurring call to live these kind of eucharistic lives.

Finally, our observation of the Lord's Supper takes as its source the Last Supper, the final meal that Jesus shared with his disciples before going to the cross. But that supper was actually, as Jamie Smith has said, "the penultimate supper."[29] It pointed ahead to another meal, a future meal. In Luke's Gospel we read, "And he said to them, 'I have eagerly desired to eat this Passover with you before I suffer. For I tell you, I will not eat it again until it finds fulfillment in the kingdom of God'" (Luke 22:15-16). The past supper was the meal of promise. The future supper will be the meal of fulfillment. Our regular participation in the Lord's Supper in the meantime is meant to make us hunger all the more as we wait for the meal that lies ahead, when God's personal presence, God's just reign and God's perfect peace will be realized in their fullness.

Being sent on God's mission. The final movement of the church's liturgy has traditionally been the sending. While this may seem at first glance to be something of an afterthought, it is in fact a crucial aspect of the logic of the liturgy. It is not merely the dismissal, not just the moment we're told, "We're finished here. You may leave now." It is instead the moment we're sent into the world to live into the story we've just rehearsed with the God we've celebrated and with whom we have communed. In fact, the word still used by Roman Catholics to refer to their worship gatherings—the word *mass*—is etymologically connected to the word *missio*. In an important sense, the whole point of the gathering is for the sending. Having breathed in, we're prepared for the breathing out. One ancient prayer from the end of the liturgy captures the sentiment well: "And now, Father, send us out to do the work you have given us to do."

Shabbat Shalom

Practicing the Vision in Sabbath Rest

The Sabbath opens creation for its true future.
On the Sabbath the redemption of the world is celebrated in anticipation.
The Sabbath is itself the presence of eternity in time,
and a foretaste of the world to come.

JÜRGEN MOLTMANN

The seventh day is the armistice in man's cruel struggle for existence,
a truce in all conflicts, personal and social, peace between
man and man, man and nature,ⁱ peace within man.

ABRAHAM JOSHUA HESCHEL

In 1909 an Italian poet named Filippo Tommaso Marinetti composed what he called "The Futurist Manifesto." Among the affirmations Marinetti penned was one that stated, "We affirm that the world's magnificence has been enriched by a new beauty: the beauty of speed."[1] Marinetti and his fellow futurists could not have imagined the myriad ways in which this "new beauty" would transform life and culture in the century after they issued their declaration. They celebrated with anticipation the potential progress of an increasingly technological society and the great promise of "more, better, faster" held out by the machine.

But for all the advantages that are ours because of our increased speed, it isn't the case that speed has always been beautiful. Faster hasn't always meant "more" or "better," especially when it comes to the things that really matter—things like friendship, family and the soul. As journalist Carl Honoré has said in his book *In Praise of Slowness*, "The problem is that our love of speed, our obsession with doing more and more in less and less time, has gone too far; it has turned into an addiction, a kind of idolatry."[2] And the more we've followed after the idol of speed, the less human we've become.

Eighty years after the futurists issued their manifesto, another movement emerged with a radically different vision of the relationship between speed and the "good life." The slow food movement officially began when delegates from fifteen countries endorsed the "Slow Food Manifesto," written by founding member Folco Portinari, on December 10, 1989. The opening lines of the manifesto read as follows:

> Our century, which began and has developed under the insignia of industrial civilization, first invented the machine and then took it as its life model.
>
> We are enslaved by speed and have all succumbed to the same insidious virus: *Fast Life.* . . .
>
> To be worthy of the name, *Homo Sapiens* should rid himself of speed before it reduces him to a species in danger of extinction.[3]

Where the futurists once saw "the beauty of speed" the advocates of the slow food movement now see an "insidious virus." Our best efforts to go faster seem to backfire on us. The proliferation of "labor-saving devices" has only made us busier. As our cars and roadways get better we drive farther and farther, spending more time and money on our commutes. The faster our computers operate, the more time we seem to spend in front of them. Our gadgets condition us to expect instant gratification, but our gratification is short-lived. All of this living at the pace of "fast life" leaves us increasingly impoverished spiritually and relationally. In 1982 a physician named Larry Dossey coined the expression "time-sickness" to describe the obsessive belief that "time is getting away, that there isn't enough of it, and that you must pedal faster and faster to keep up."[4] Today we all seem to suffer from time-sickness. As an *Adbusters* article called "The Slow Lane" puts it,

> Our faith that faster equals better has buried our speedometer and made us relate to time like a lab rat relates to cocaine. Surrounded by a blitzkrieg of cell phones, microprocessor upon microprocessor, four hours of TV a day, always-on internet, eight-lane highways, 50-hour work weeks, drive-thru culture and "just-in-time" economies, it's little wonder we crave time more than anything else.[5]

We've forgotten how to inhabit time in ways that are fully human. For this, we need to recover the Sabbath.

One of the most important disciplines we can retrieve in order to shape and sustain life with God for the world is the discipline of Sabbath keeping. But I must confess at the outset of this chapter that that's a sentence I never thought I'd write. For a long time the very mention of the discipline of Sabbath keeping caused my shoulders to tense up and my blood pressure to rise. My visceral reaction to Sabbath was born of two deeply held (if never articulated) perceptions. On the one hand, I avoided thinking about, reading about, hearing about or talking about Sabbath because my life felt so busy that the notion of carving out a completely unproductive twenty-four-hour period seemed beyond my ability even to entertain. With all of the demands that come with holding down two jobs, my work inevitably bled over into "the rest of life." Even when I was able to set aside my professional responsibilities on the weekends, I had things to do around the house that required my time and exertion. To keep Sabbath was simply not a possibility. Thus any mention of Sabbath evoked a sense of guilt in me; I knew it was something I was supposed to be pursuing, but it seemed utterly impossible to put in to practice in my hurried life.

I also avoided Sabbath because there was nothing in my understanding of it that attracted me to it. My perceptions were entirely negative, shaped only by what I understood to be its prohibitions. When I thought of Sabbath I thought only of what you can't do, and most of the things I thought you couldn't do were things I wanted to do or felt like I needed to do. Sabbath sounded more like misery than time well spent. "Perhaps," I thought, "it's supposed to feel that way. Perhaps it's a kind of discipline of mortification, a practice of dying to yourself." I associated Sabbath more with death than with life.

I took comfort in knowing there was no New Testament reiteration of the command to keep the Sabbath. I also knew that Paul's words in Colossians 2:16-17 made it clear that Christians were not to judge one another on the basis of "what you eat or drink, or with regard to a religious festival, a New Moon celebration or a Sabbath day." I knew Sabbath was a sign of the Old Covenant, a strict commandment for those under that covenant. I found relief in knowing that Christians were no longer bound by the Old Covenant requirements. I had not yet come to understand the reality that Dan Allender captures so well when he writes, "A commandment is often assumed merely to be a prohibition. Such thinking is idiocy. God's commandments prevent us from sucking diesel fumes in order to orient us to delicious, fresh air. Sabbath is the healthiest air for us to breathe."[6] I had become caught up in the cultural cult of productivity. I was sucking diesel fumes and I didn't even know it. Or I didn't want to admit it. In my heart I knew things were off kilter. Though I couldn't name my condition, I had a sense of being "time-sick." What I did not know was how much I needed the delicious, fresh air of Sabbath.

Over the past few years I've become a student and an (uneven) observer of the Sabbath. And I've come to discover that Sabbath is not so much about dying to self but about becoming fully alive. It's not about drudgery but about delight. It's not about doing nothing but about engaging something that shapes and sustains life with God for the world. Sabbath keeping is a spiritual practice that is deeply in tune with the vision of God. It's about experiencing God's presence, inhabiting God's reign and anticipating God's perfect peace. As Allender says, "Sabbath is holy time where we feast, play, dance, have sex, sing, pray, laugh, tell stories, read, paint, walk, and watch creation in its fullness. Few people are willing to enter the Sabbath and sanctify it, to make it holy, because a full day of delight and joy is more than most people can bear in a lifetime, let alone a week."[7] Jesus said, "The Sabbath was made for humankind" (Mark 2:27 NRSV). It was made for our delight, our joy, our flourishing. It was made for us to enjoy the God who creates and sustains life, to gather with friends in order to "taste and see that the LORD is good" (Psalm 34:8) and to fashion foretastes of the world to come.

The Co-optation of the Sabbath

Before proceeding to explore the Christian practice of Sabbath keeping, it's worth pointing out the ways in which this practice has been rediscovered and reappropriated for a different set of purposes in our contemporary cultural environment. More and more people are beginning to recognize the way that "time-sickness" is adversely affecting us all. Therefore, as Lauren Winner has noted, "The Sabbath has come back into fashion, even among the most secular Americans." But the "Sabbath" that many seem to be embracing is a curious one. Winner writes, "Articles abound extolling the virtues of treating yourself to a day of rest, a relaxing and leisurely visit to the spa, an extra-long bubble bath, and a glass of Chardonnay. Take a day off, the magazines urge their harried readers. Rest."[8] Winner identifies two fundamental flaws in the secular co-optation of Sabbath. The first is what she calls "capitalism's justification for Sabbath rest," which is the notion that resting one day a week will make you more productive during the other six. While it may be true that our productivity the other six days is enhanced by the practice of a day of rest, this instrumental view of the Sabbath runs counter to the biblical logic of Sabbath keeping. This view exalts the popular anthropology running deep within contemporary Western culture that says human beings are fundamentally beings that produce and beings that consume. Sabbath keeping in this view is a means to achieving the end of making us better producers and therefore more able consumers.

Winner's insights echo those of notable Jewish author Abraham Joshua Heschel, who decades earlier in his classic book *The Sabbath* wrote, "To the biblical mind . . . the Sabbath as a day of rest, as a day of abstaining from toil, is not for the purpose of recovering one's lost strength and becoming fit for the forthcoming labor. The Sabbath is a day for the sake of life. Man is not a beast of burden, and the Sabbath is not for the purpose of enhancing the efficiency of his work."[9] Heschel turns this instrumental way of thinking on it head when he writes, "The Sabbath is not for the sake of the weekdays; the weekdays are for the sake of the Sabbath. It is not an interlude but the climax of living."[10]

In the Genesis story, God did not rest on the seventh day because he was weary from all his labor and needed a breather so he'd be up to the tasks that lay ahead. Rest has a deeper meaning than merely a recharge of the batteries for the sake of what's next. God rested to let the world he had made flourish as it should. He rested in order to delight in its flourishing. The word "rest" that occurs in the Genesis story and elsewhere with reference to the Sabbath is the Hebrew word *menuha*. According to Heschel, "To the biblical mind *menuha* is the same as happiness and stillness, as peace and harmony. . . . It is the state in which there is not strife and no fighting, no fear and no distrust. The essence of good life is *menuha*."[11] Capitalism's justification of the Sabbath says that the essence of the good life is increased capacity for production and consumption and that a day of rest is a useful means to that end. Biblical thinking about the Sabbath runs in precisely the opposite direction.

The second flaw in the secular co-optation of the Sabbath that Winner identifies is what she calls "the fallacy of the direct object." Winner writes, "Whom is the contemporary Sabbath designed to honor? Whom does it benefit? Why, the bubble-bath taker herself, of course! The Bible suggests something different. In observing the Sabbath, one is both giving a gift to God and imitating Him."[12] If not understood and engaged rightly, Sabbath keeping can become just another form of narcissistic self-indulgence. That is not to say that there are not great personal benefits to be gained and great personal joys to be experienced in keeping Sabbath. There certainly are. It is simply to say that whatever benefit, joy, delight and renewal we experience come not because we pursued these as ends within themselves. Rather, we receive them as gifts and means of grace that come as we pursue God in the keeping of Sabbath.

Dwelling in Sabbath Time

In order to understand how the Christian practice of keeping Sabbath shapes and sustains our life with God for the world, we need to see how this practice is grounded in three great events in the grand narrative of Scripture. Each of these events offers a slightly different perspective on our understanding of and engagement in the observance of Sabbath. They are creation, exodus and resurrection.

Creation: Inhabiting the sovereignty of God. The Sabbath command is first given to Israel in Exodus 20:8-11:

> Remember the Sabbath day by keeping it holy. Six days you shall
> labor and do all your work, but the seventh day is a Sabbath to

the Lord your God. On it you shall not do any work, neither you, nor your son or daughter, nor your male or female servant, nor your animals, nor any foreigner residing in your towns. For in six days the Lord made the heavens and the earth, the sea, and all that is in them, but he rested on the seventh day. Therefore the Lord blessed the Sabbath day and made it holy.

Here the command to rest is grounded in God's act of creation and his rest on the seventh day. In both our work and our rest, we image God. But our obedience to his command to keep the Sabbath is one of the most important ways we can be reminded that, while we image God, we're not him. In keeping Sabbath we "acknowledge the limits of our humanness."[13]

Unlike the utilitarian approaches to Sabbath discussed above, the point of Sabbath keeping from a biblical perspective is found precisely in its uselessness, its sheer impracticality. It is a way of inhabiting the sovereignty of God, a regular reminder that it is God who created and sustains the world and that it will continue to go on spinning whether or not I lift a finger. In Sabbath I'm reminded that the world's maintenance does not depend on me. Sabbath reminds me that God is infinite and I am finite. God is powerful and I am weak. God is self-sufficient and I am dependent. God is all things to all people and I am tiny in comparison to him. This is crucial because many of us live as though we don't know our limits, as though we don't want to acknowledge having any. We cling to the sense that we are indispensable. Israel practiced Sabbath—and we do as well—to be reminded that God cares for his creation and that he provides for his people. The regular practice of Sabbath helps cure us of our Promethean tendency to overreach our limits. As Ruth Haley Barton writes, "There is a freedom that comes from being who we are in God and resting in God that eventually enables us to bring something truer to the world than all our doing."[14]

Exodus: Inhabiting the justice of God. The Sabbath command is reiterated to Israel before they enter the Promised Land in Deuteronomy 5:12-15. In this restatement of the command, attention is drawn not to creation but to God's mighty act in delivering his people from Egypt:

> Observe the Sabbath day by keeping it holy, as the LORD your God has commanded you. Six days you shall labor and do all your work, but the seventh day is a sabbath to the LORD your God. On it you shall not do any work, neither you, nor your son or daughter, nor your male or female servant, nor your ox, your donkey or any of your animals, nor any foreigner residing in your towns, so that your male and female servants may rest, as you do. Remember that you were slaves in Egypt and that the LORD your God brought you out of there with a mighty hand and an outstretched arm. Therefore the LORD your God has commanded you to observe the Sabbath day.

"Remember that you were slaves." The focus of the Sabbath command in Deuteronomy is on inhabiting the liberating justice of God. The people of Israel were called to remember what it meant to be slaves and what it felt like to be liberated. The practice of Sabbath called them to practice liberation. Dorothy Bass writes, "Slaves cannot take a day off; free people can. When they stop work every seventh day, the people will remember that the Lord brought them out of slavery, and they will see to it that no one within their dominion, not even animals, will work without respite. Sabbath rest is a recurring testimony against the drudgery of slavery."[15]

This reiteration of the Sabbath command reminds us that the practice of Sabbath is not only for our own personal benefit but is designed to benefit everyone. We are not only to cease our own work, but we're to relinquish the demand that anyone else work on our behalf. Sabbath is about human flourishing. Not just my flourishing, but our flourishing. Human flourishing. In fact, Deuteronomy tells us, it's about all creation flourishing. Inhabiting the justice of God includes rest for "your ox, your donkey, and any of your animals." Sabbath was one of the practices that God intended to ensure that the people of Israel were a people of justice.

Resurrection: Inhabiting the dream of God for a world set right. In Isaiah 58:13-14 we find the explicit connection between the observance of Sabbath and the experience of joy and delight:

> If you keep your feet from breaking the Sabbath
> and from doing as you please on my holy day,
> if you call the Sabbath a delight
> and the LORD's holy day honorable,
> and if you honor it by not going your own way
> and not doing as you please or speaking idle words,
> then you will find your joy in the LORD.

This passage challenges the common assumption that Sabbath is merely a time of negative rules and restrictions, a day of suffocating obligations and prohibitions, a day without play or pleasure. Instead the poet says we must "call the Sabbath a delight." Drawing on the work of ancient rabbis, Heschel writes,

> Call the Sabbath a delight: a delight to the soul and a delight to the body. Since there are so many acts which one must abstain from doing on the seventh day, "you might think I have given you the Sabbath for your displeasure; I have surely given you the Sabbath for your pleasure." To sanctify the seventh day does not mean: Thou shalt mortify thyself, but, on the contrary: Thou shalt sanctify it with all thy heart, with all thy soul and with all thy senses. "Sanctify the Sabbath by choice meals, by beautiful garments; delight your soul with pleasure and I will reward you for this very pleasure."[16]

This emphasis on joy and delight is grounded in eschatology, the dream of God for a world set right. As Heschel rightly insists, "The Sabbath is a reminder of the two worlds—this world and the world to come; it is an example of both worlds."[17] For the Christian this hope for the world to come is secured by our faith in the resurrection of Jesus. In the Easter event, the world to come has broken in on this world. In practicing the Sabbath—eating choice food, drinking good wine, laughing, telling stories, enjoying leisurely conversation and communion—we fashion foretastes of the world to come. As Dan Allender writes, "The Sabbath is a day when the kingdom to come has come and is celebrated now rather than anticipated tomorrow. It is a fiction, a theater of divine comedy that practices eternity as a present reality rather than a future state."[18] In Sabbath, we practice new creation. We inhabit resurrection. We taste, touch, hear, feel and smell the hors d'oeuvres of the banquet that awaits us. We get foretastes of shalom.

Practicing the Sabbath

My family has been attempting to recover the observance of Sabbath with varying degrees of success over the last couple of years. We haven't exactly mastered the art of Sabbath keeping, but there have been a number of practices and priorities that we've found helpful along the way. We generally practice Sabbath from dinnertime on Friday evening until the same time on Saturday. This is in keeping with the ancient Jewish custom of marking the beginning of the day with sundown instead of sunrise. This allows us to prepare a meal before the Sabbath begins and to enjoy a leisurely evening of good food and good conversation around the dinner table before heading off to an early bedtime. Sometimes we shift and begin on Saturday evening so that we can have our Sabbath observance correspond with the day we gather with our community for worship. This follows the ancient Christian pattern of commemorating the resurrection of Jesus on the first day of the week. But because I am a pastor, Sundays are often workdays for me, so more often than not our Sabbath spans from Friday to Saturday. I'm not convinced that the particular day we carve out matters nearly as much as that we do in fact carve out a day. We're not rigid or legalistic about our observance of the Sabbath, but we have chosen to prioritize engaging rest, delight and connection and disengaging productivity, commerce and technology.

Engage rest. Abraham Joshua Heschel calls the Sabbath "an opportunity to mend our tattered lives."[19] We can begin to do this first by engaging sacred rest. The biblical notion of Sabbath rest is, as has been said, rooted in God's rest on the seventh day in the Genesis creation account. There God's rest is depicted not as his crumpling in exhaustion after a taxing week of work. It is not a twenty-four-hour nap for him to recharge his batteries. And it is not a time where he sits around twiddling his thumbs, eager to get back to work once his self-imposed day of boredom has come and gone. In his day of rest God watches and enjoys creation's flourishing. God enters into the joy of creation as it's meant to be and quietly celebrates its glory.

To enter into Sabbath rest is not to do nothing. Rest in this rich sense does not necessarily imply a cessation of all activity. It is instead to enter into flourishing, to engage the things that give us life, that stir our souls, that help us thrive as the kind of beings God has created us to be. It is to set aside achieving and to simply enjoy being. To enter into Sabbath rest is to inhabit time differently. It is to let go of the need to watch the clock, to move a bit more slowly through the day, to pay more attention to what's happening around us and within us than "fast life" usually allows. Often for me it means good coffee, an old book, an overstuffed chair and some Miles Davis. It frequently means sleeping in, a walk through the park near our home and a nice midafternoon nap. It means taking time to be quiet and be still. In the rest of Sabbath—the stillness and quiet both within and without—we experience the nearness of God and have our souls renewed by him. In his book *The Rest of God*, Mark

Buchanan says, "In a culture where busyness is a fetish and stillness is laziness, rest is sloth. But without rest, we miss the rest of God: the rest he invites us to enter more fully so that we might know him more deeply. . . . Some knowing is never pursued, only received. And for that, you need to be still."[20] Sabbath allows us the time to pay attention and to open ourselves to what God wants to do in us.

Engage delight. The second way we mend our tattered lives on the Sabbath is by intentionally engaging delight. As Isaiah 58:13-14 makes explicitly clear, finding our joy in the Lord is bound up with calling the Sabbath a delight. To flourish as the kinds of beings God made us to be is to experience the beauty and goodness of life and creation with all the power of our senses. A spirituality that is creation affirming, people affirming and body affirming is a sensual spirituality. But as Dan Allender has perceptively noted,

> Somewhere along the way, there has been a tragic division between holiness and sensuality. It is the work of evil to divide, and it must be fought directly and sensually. God stood back from each day of creation and declared that it was good. God called what he saw beautiful in that everything he created revealed something different about his glory.[21]

God intends the goodness and beauty in creation and culture to stir our affections for him. He shines in all that's fair. On the Sabbath we are to "bask in beauty, to surround our senses with color, texture, taste, fragrance, fire, sound, sweetness, and delight."[22]

The problem comes from the ways we have numbed ourselves to the experience of holy delight. In his book *Living the Sabbath*, Norman Wirzba suggests that the success of today's entertainment industry is the clearest indication that our culture is becoming increasingly incapable of experiencing genuine delight. While this may seem counterintuitive, since entertainment and delight seem to be near synonyms, I think Wirzba's contention is entirely correct. He writes, "The at-

traction of many forms of entertainment . . . is that they give us release
or escape from life, whereas the experience of delight follows from a
deeper immersion and affirmation of it."[23] We often settle for shallow
facsimiles of delight that come easily to us rather than giving ourselves
to the effort it takes to find what brings us true delight.

In our family observance of the Sabbath we splurge for the sake of
delight. Flowers for the table. The nice dishes. A scrumptious meal
enjoyed with family and friends. Root beer and ice cream for the kids.
Dark chocolate and the good coffee for the grownups. To "keep the
Sabbath holy" is to experience it as set apart from the mundane. It is
to pay attention to the details. Sabbath asks us to observe, to take
notice and to savor the particulars, to be fully present in this place, at
this moment, with these people. As we engage the things that bring
us delight, we remember the joy of Eden and anticipate the joy of the
new heavens and new earth.

Engage connection. One of the greatest sources of delight in our
family's practice of Sabbath is the opportunity it affords us to forge
and foster deep connection with one another and with our friends.
Sabbath is a day for life together. If Sabbath is a day to flourish as the
beings God made us to be, it's imperative that we remember on that
day that he has made us for each other; he has made us for intimate
connection. According to St. Augustine, two things in this world are
essential: life and friendship. God has given us life and desires that we
experience it in its fullness. But to experience it in its fullness means
to experience it with friends. Augustine writes,

> Good human beings seem even in this life to provide no small
> consolation. For, if poverty pinches, if grief saddens, if bodily
> pain disturbs, if exile discourages, if any other disaster torments,
> provided there are present human beings who not only know
> how to rejoice with those in joy, but also to weep with those who
> weep (Rom 12:15) and can speak and converse in a helpful way,

those rough spots are smoothed, the heavy burdens are lightened, and adversity is overcome.[24]

A bit further on he concludes, "In no human affairs is anything dear to a human being without a friend." God has made us to experience the fullness of life in intimate connection with family and friends, and we nurture those bonds as we together "taste and see that the Lord is good" in our shared experience of Sabbath.

We spend more time together around the table on our Sabbath day than any other day during the week. As will be discussed further in the next chapter, the table is the central place of connection, so for us it plays a central role in our experience of Sabbath. When friends join us for dinner for the first time on an evening that begins the Sabbath for us, we have to explain why we light a special candle and say a special prayer, and it opens up great conversation about the beauty of Sabbath keeping in a time-sick world. Not all of our friends who have tasted of the Sabbath with us have adopted our practice as their own. But they all leave having glimpsed Sabbath delight.

Our observance of Sabbath has been richly rewarding for our connectedness as a family. We pull out all our favorite board games, spend time outside doing things we love together or just sit together and talk. So much of our time during the week is spent shuffling around from one activity to another that we rarely have the time and space to engage one another at much more than a superficial level. And even when we do, we find ourselves easily distracted by our many devices. In keeping Sabbath, we disengage from the many things that normally inhibit our ability to connect.

Disengage productivity. Engaging rest, delight and connection requires some corresponding disengagement. One of the most challenging aspects of Sabbath keeping for many of us is its demand that we disengage productivity. For many of us, accomplishment and productivity have become more than the means of our livelihood and have become instead the meaning of our lives. Achievement, success, accolades and advancement have become some of the most persistent yet also the most subtle idols to which we turn, broken cisterns we run back to time and again. And these idols are no less pernicious than those Israel stubbornly ran after. They are just more tasteful and discreet. Our idols have become more sophisticated, but they demand our worship and our sacrifice. Many of us have learned to cope with the vandalism of shalom by burying ourselves in our work, finding there a sense of security, identity and meaning and a place to hide from vulnerability and suffering.

To enter into Sabbath rest is an act of repentance and faith. It is a means by which we practice the reality that we are truly beggars, that we know ourselves to be created and sustained by the grace of God rather than our own strength and ingenuity. This requires that we repent of the idolatry of productivity. It requires that we acknowledge that we are more than what we do, that our identity is greater than the sum of our accomplishments, and that our security is not found in the strength of our own hands. To cease striving—to relinquish achieving and embrace being—is an act of faith. Sabbath is an embodied reminder that there is a God and we're not him. It calls us to acknowledge the limits of our humanness and to trust in the sustaining grace and mercy of God.

To enter the Sabbath with repentance and faith opens us to experience it as a gift and means of grace as we experience the renewing presence of God. We are not to work on the Sabbath because to do so would take us out of our experience of joy, celebration and delight. Dan Allender offers a memorable analogy for understanding just how out of place working on the Sabbath is. He writes, "It is as bizarre as making love to your spouse, but getting out of bed during the process to cut your lawn or wash dishes. Such an offense would do far more than spoil the mood; it would be a direct assault on the integrity of joy, announcing that a mundane chore is more pleasurable than sexual joy with your spouse."[25] Only by disengaging productivity can we fully experience the glory that the Sabbath has to offer—to taste, touch, see, hear and smell the glimpses of shalom that make up our Sabbath joy.

Disengage commerce. Another act of disengagement required of us if Sabbath is to become a means of mending our tattered lives is disengagement from commerce. Again, Sabbath is intended for the flourishing of all creation. For me to cease working but to demand that others work on my behalf makes Sabbath about my own self-fulfillment. The command to keep Sabbath in Deuteronomy 5 called the people of Israel not only to stop their own work but also to relinquish others—whether people or animals—from the burden of working for their benefit.

Sabbath is a weekly rhythm through which we learn to extricate ourselves from the pervasiveness and power of consumerism. As Walter Brueggemann has perceptively put it, consumerism operates on the claim that "'more is better,' that 'most' will make happy, and that each is entitled to and must have all that each can take, even at the expense of others."[26] Like productivity, consumption has become one of the more persistent of the tasteful, discreet idols of our day. Rather than consuming to live, we're increasingly living to consume, finding our sense of self in the things we acquire or the ability to acquire things. In a consumer culture all of life becomes framed in terms of consumer choice. All of these choices are framed by the question "what's in it for me?" Consumerism is the exploitation of the incurvature of the soul for economic gain. And it's the water we're all swimming in.

In a consumer culture we are particularly prone to the manipulation of desire. The whole system of consumerism rests on its power to create in us a tenacious insatiability. It hangs on what Rodney Clapp has called "the deification of dissatisfaction."[27] The seemingly endless barrage of commercial messages and images we encounter every day in every sphere of our lives reinforces in us the sense that we are lacking. Marketers then preach the gospel of their products, attempting to convince us that what seems like a God-shaped hole can actually be filled by a simple purchase. As one astute observer of consumerism has put it, this pseudo-gospel holds out the hope that, if we embrace it, our life may one day be "on earth as it is in advertising."[28] The next purchase never gives us the life we want in its fullness. But the evangelists of consumerism stand at the ready to offer us another product.

Sabbath keeping helps us curb this sense of dissatisfaction that all too easily grips our hearts. It is a once-a-week, twenty-four-hour consumer detox. It helps us practice gratitude and contentment, the bitter enemies of consumerism. It teaches us to delight more in people than in things, in creation rather than consumption and, ultimately, to delight in God and to rest our identity in him.

Disengage technology. Finally, for our family at least, Sabbath means disengaging from technology. In her book *The Winter of Our Disconnect*, Susan Maushart tells of her dawning recognition of the invasiveness of technology in her life and that of her family. She describes one example after another of the ways her teenage children's lives were becoming dominated by their devices. But then she had her own personal epiphany:

> It wasn't until I started surfing the Net, replying to text messages, listening to podcasts, and, on one memorable occasion, doing a live radio interview—all the while "otherwise engaged" in the loo—that I admitted I had a problem. Was I was using media to (cringe) self-medicate, on the fast track to becoming a middle-aged Lindsay Lohan of the App Store? Was it time to check myself in to rehab?[29]

The rest of Maushart's book is the winsome tale of how she led her family into a digital "wilderness wandering," going off the technological grid for six months. With candor and wit she narrates the lessons they learned about themselves and their technology along the way. She offers an insightful tale to help us navigate life in an increasingly tech-saturated society.

Arthur Paul Boers has perceptively observed that "when we allow devices and machines to reside at the center of our lives, we displace values and practices that once enriched the quality of how we live. We end up serving our gadgets instead of using them as tools to support our priorities."[30] Recognizing the way this pattern was playing out in the life of my own family played a large part in our decision to disengage technology as a crucial part of our Sabbath observance.

Like most adolescent boys in our culture, my oldest son has a deep affinity for his devices. He divides his time fairly evenly between the television, the computer, the video game console and my smart phone. So I gave him quite a shock the first time I told him our family was going to practice a twenty-four-hour Sabbath and that I wanted us to "unplug" for an entire day. My request seemed altogether unreasonable in his mind. But I was beginning to see just how invasive technology had become in our lives and how much it was distracting us from one another. I wanted us to disengage from it so that we could really engage one another. My son begrudgingly obliged.

To his surprise and mine, it didn't take long for him to recognize that disengaging from technology had its benefits. While it meant that he couldn't be distracted by his devices, it also meant I couldn't be distracted by mine. We interacted with one another and the rest of the family that day in ways that we hadn't in a long time. By the middle of the day on Saturday he said to me, "Maybe this Sabbath thing isn't such a bad idea after all." But by the end of our twenty-four hours, he said, "I think Sabbath may be the best idea since technology." That weekend I became more aware than ever not just how dependent my kids were on technology but how much it had come to dominate my life.

I don't have a Bible verse to back up my appeal to unplug from technology in the observance of Sabbath. But I do know that part of keeping Sabbath is learning to inhabit time in a way that's fully human, to be present in the present. And I know that technology can undermine my ability to do that. As with all other aspects of our practice of

Sabbath keeping, we don't become absolutist or legalistic about disengaging technology. We simply choose to turn off and put away whatever we think will inhibit us from fully participating in rest, delight and connection. This has become for us a crucial part of what it means to "keep the Sabbath holy."

The customary greeting in Israel to this day when you meet someone on the Sabbath is "shabbat shalom"—Sabbath peace. In that greeting we're reminded of Sabbath's purpose. To practice Sabbath is to practice shalom, to rehearse the way things are supposed to be. Weekly Sabbath keeping is a rhythm of remembrance and anticipation—looking back to creation and ahead to the renewal of all things. As we practice Sabbath we live into the vision of God. We delight in his nearness to us as we pay attention to him through keeping the Sabbath holy. We inhabit his just reign now in anticipation of its coming consummation. We experience foretastes of the perfect peace we will one day enjoy as we relish the fleeting glimpses of the rest, delight and connection we were created to enjoy and now wait for in hope.

Table Manners

Practicing the Vision Through Feasting and Fasting

When Jesus himself wanted to explain to his disciples
what his forthcoming death was all about, he didn't
give them a theory, he gave them a meal.

N. T. WRIGHT

Blessed are you, O Lord God, King of the Universe, for you give
us food to sustain our lives and make our hearts glad.

THE BOOK OF COMMON PRAYER

The average human being has about ten thousand taste buds. The only conceivable explanation I can think of for why that would be is that God loves us. Really loves us. Think of the most delicious meal you can remember. Whether it was at a fancy French restaurant or your grandmother's dining room table, it was a symphony of pleasure for all ten thousand of your taste buds. And it didn't have to be that way. God did not have to make us capable of experiencing such culinary delight. He could have made us the sort of creatures for whom food is merely fuel. But he didn't do that because of his great love for us.

Our ten thousand taste buds are a means of gastronomic grace. He shines in all that's fair.

Chances are good that your most memorable meal was shared with others around a table. Tables are one of the most fundamental things that make us human. No other animal eats at a table. And tables remind us that for humans, eating is not just about fuel. Sharing a table is one of the most vital means of human connection. We are often most fully alive when we're sharing a table. That's why it should come as no surprise that throughout the pages of the Scriptures, God shows up at tables. And at the center of the spiritual life of both the Old and the New Testament people of God stands a table: the table of the Passover and the table of the Lord's Supper. Several of Jesus' postresurrection appearances involve sharing food—in the upper room in Jerusalem, at the table in Emmaus and on the shore of the Sea of Galilee.

Eating and sex are the two most intense sensual experiences God has given us to enjoy. And both are intended not only to give us the experience of sensual pleasure but also to offer us a window into the heart of the life-giving God who dreamed them up. Is it any wonder then that both have become so destructively spoiled by evil? If the biblical story is true and there is a will at work in the world that wants to thwart God's intention for his good creation, it should come as no surprise that these two beautiful gifts of God would be twisted by evil to bring us shame and disgrace. As Christopher West has said, "If we want to know what is most sacred in the world, all we need to do is look for what is most violently profaned."[1]

You don't have to look far to see that contemporary North American culture suffers from a kind of collective eating disorder. From the epidemic of obesity on the one hand to the approximately twenty-four million lives wracked by disorders such as anorexia and bulimia on the other, it's plain to see that our culture has a problem with food. An embodied spirituality informed by the logic of the incarnation has to take food seriously. There are two historical Christian practices that help us to do just that: feasting and fasting. A careful reader of the Gospels will note how frequently both of these practices show up in the accounts of the life and ministry of Jesus. Recovering an understanding of and engagement in these two disciplines is essential for shaping and sustaining life with God for the world.

To Feast or to Fast?

In Luke 5—immediately following a scene revolving around a dinner party—Jesus is confronted by a group of religious leaders who question him about the practice of fasting among his followers. "They said to him, 'John's disciples often fast and pray, and so do the disciples of the Pharisees, but yours go on eating and drinking'" (Luke 5:33). Among the most notable and highly criticized aspects of Jesus' ministry were his eating habits and those of his disciples. Apparently they were choosing not to follow the frequent patterns of fasting that were characteristic of the followers of John the Baptist and the Pharisees. When asked to explain the reason for their apparent preference for feasting over fasting, Jesus said, "Can you make the friends of the bridegroom fast while he is with them? But the time will come when the bridegroom will be taken from them; in those days they will fast" (Luke 5:34). A wedding was the biggest excuse for a party in the lives of the people of the ancient Mediterranean world. The expression Jesus uses that is translated as "friends of the bridegroom" refers literally to those who were responsible for the party. Jesus (in keeping with Jewish tradition) frequently used the images of a wedding, a bride and a bridegroom as metaphors for the kingdom of God. Here Jesus says, when the bridegroom is present it's a time for feasting, not fasting. As the Old Testament prophets had said, when the reign of God comes it will be marked by an endless messianic banquet.

This was the very reason John the Baptist was so well known for fasting instead of feasting. John and his disciples fasted in anticipation, groaning for the coming kingdom of God, the coming messianic banquet. John's fasts were a protest against the world remaining as it was and a physical plea for God to decisively show up and establish his uncontested reign. John fasted for the kingdom to come. Jesus feasted because in him it had. So where does that leave us? We live in the time between the advents, between Christ's first coming in humility and his second coming in glory. In Jesus' incarnation, the reign of God burst into the dominion of sin, death and the devil. His first advent was the inbreaking of the kingdom. His second advent will bring its consummation. We live in the tension between time when the kingdom has already broken in and not yet come in its fullness. Christ has come, so we feast. Christ is yet to come again, so we fast.[2] And as we live in the time of the already—not yet kingdom of God, we need to recover both feasting and fasting as defiant practices, communal practices and eschatological practices.

Feasting and the Vision of God

When I speak of feasting, I don't have in mind what we often mean when we use the word—namely, an excuse for overindulgence. To talk about feasting in a Christian sense is not to talk primarily about the amount of food we eat but the manner in which we eat it. But it should be pointed out from the beginning of the discussion that many of us live such overindulgent lives that we are incapable of really feasting. As some of my creative friends are prone to say, "When everything is bold, nothing is bold." When our appetites are habitually overindulged, our ability to experience a meal as a feast is undermined. Feasting loses its meaning in a culture of gluttony.

When I speak of feasting in a Christian sense—as a spiritual discipline—I mean simply a special meal enjoyed as a gift and means of grace. There are things to be said that must be said elsewhere about the spiritual significance of our everyday meals (for they are significant indeed). But what I have in view here are special meals, those meals where we savor in a special way not only the food and conversation but also the goodness and presence of God. They need not be lavish meals. They can in fact be quite simple. But they are meals where we gather with guests around a table and get a glimpse of the banquet of the kingdom, those meals where we get a little foretaste of shalom. They are those meals that are our "thin places." Michael Frost writes,

> The Celts speak of "thin places," where the fabric that separates heaven and earth is so thin it becomes almost translucent and one is able to encounter the joy and peace of heaven. In the Celtic tradition, such places give us an opening into the magnificence and wonder of the world to come. . . . To them a thin place is where the veil that separates heaven and earth is lifted and one is able to receive a glimpse of the glory of God.[3]

For me the veil is thin when I'm seated at the table with good food and cherished friends.

While I was writing this chapter, my family made the very difficult decision that it was time to have our thirteen-year-old border collie put to sleep. She was a beloved member of our family, a part of each of my children's lives from the time they were born. I took her to the vet, sat with her cross-legged on the floor and bawled my eyes out. When I got home, two of our dearest friends were there with dinner. Their presence and that meal were a gift of grace on what was a painful day for us. As we sat down to eat, we raised our glasses and I said, "God, we thank you that there is coming a day when all that is wrong will be made right, all that is broken will be made whole, and all that is marred will be made beautiful. And we thank you for glimpses of that day as we share good food with good friends." We all dabbed our wet faces and ate, savoring our meal and our time together. They stayed for hours, but the time flew by. It was for us a feast, a thin place.

Feasting is not a practice that makes it onto a lot of the lists of the classic disciplines of the Christian life. But I'm convinced it's a fundamentally important practice and one that desperately needs to be recovered in our day. To practice feasting as a Christian spiritual discipline helps us undo some of the toxic effects of our contemporary cultural environment. It helps us connect more deeply in Christian community and with our not-yet-Christian neighbors. And it helps captivate our imagination and passion for the world to come.

Feasting as a defiant practice. In the opening chapter of the Old Testament book of Daniel we find the story of Daniel and his three friends who have been taken away from their homeland in Israel to their new home in exile in Babylon. They're subjected to a cultural reprogramming in the court of the king. They're given Babylonian names, taught Babylonian stories, immersed in Babylonian values and fed Babylonian food. They are given a new vision of "the good life" and a new set of embodied practices aimed at shaping them to love certain things and pursue certain ends. The whole project is intended to undo their enculturation as good Israelites and turn them into good Babylonians. But Daniel and his friends make one small request that is decisive for the story. They ask to be allowed to practice their peculiarity at the table, to determine their own eating habits. And this decision to eat differently from the culture seeking to shape them into its mold was an act of quiet defiance that enabled them to maintain their distinctiveness as the people of God in exile.

Arthur Paul Boers has observed that "food is an essential way for people to express their values, to live by their convictions, to uphold what they consider most vital and important."[4] This statement certainly rings true of Daniel and his friends. But if Boers is correct—and I believe that he is—what do American eating habits reveal about what we consider most vital and important? What does how we eat reflect about our values and convictions? What does it say about us that one out of every five meals Americans eat is consumed in a car, that one out of four Americans consume some type of fast food every day, and that ten percent of our disposable income is spent on fast food every year?[5] More and more of our meals are being eaten behind wheels or in front of screens. And our food choices reflect a higher value placed on cost and convenience than on other values like health, sustainability and the ethics of production. In his book *The Omnivore's Dilemma*, Michael Pollan writes, "Though much has been done to obscure this simple fact, how and what we eat determines to a great extent the use we make of the world—and what is to become of it."[6] Sadly, our collective habits seem to indicate that we don't much care about the "use we make of the world" or "what is to become of it" so long as everything we want is inexpensive and accessible.

One of the key practices we can engage to shape and sustain our life with God for the world is the practice of feasting, sharing special meals prepared and received in love with our families, friends and neighbors. Feasting can be for us a quietly defiant practice, a practice that helps us overcome the "time-sickness" that troubles so many of us. It can help us ward off the idolatry of productivity and the creeping invasiveness of technology. A feast enables us—in fact requires us—to slow down, to pay attention, to make connections. It is a way that we as Christians "express our values, to live by our convictions, to uphold what we consider most vital and important."

In the last chapter I discussed the slow food movement, a grassroots network of over 150,000 people from more than 150 countries. According to the Slow Food Manifesto, fast life has "changed our way of being and threatens our environment and our landscapes." According to the manifesto, "Our defense should begin at the table."[7] The slow food movement may have something profoundly important to teach us. According to its website, the mission of Slow Food USA is "good, clean and fair food for all."

- *Good.* Our food should be tasty, seasonal, local, fresh and wholesome.

- *Clean.* Our food should nourish a healthful lifestyle and be produced in ways that preserve biodiversity, sustain the environment and ensure animal welfare—without harming human health.

- *Fair.* Our food should be affordable by all, while respecting the dignity of labor from field to fork.

- *For all.* Good, clean and fair food should be accessible to all and celebrate the diverse cultures, traditions and nations that reside in the USA.[8]

Aren't these guidelines in keeping with the sorts of things that should be of concern to those of us learning to live into the vision of God? Thinking more carefully as Christians about the ways we eat can help us practice a distinct identity that rejects the patterns our contemporary cultural environment tries to force on us.

Feasting as a communal practice. I love to cook. Maybe I'm devoting half a chapter to feasting because I love to cook almost as much as I love to eat. I've never been much of an artist, but there's something artistic about creating a delicious meal. So for me, my kitchen is my studio, my cutting board my palette and my plate my canvas. There's something rich and rewarding to me about slicing and dicing and chopping. It calms me and centers me in ways that few other things really can. But even more than the personal pleasure I get from cooking, I delight in sharing my food with people I care about. I delight in their experience of the food I've made. Cooking is an act of love.

My family is usually not very big on celebrating New Year's Eve, but last year we decided it was a good night for a feast. We kept it small, inviting just two of our dearest friends and their three kids to join us for the night. Our friend Crystal loves to cook as much as I do, so we decided that she and I were going to team up to cook tapas—small plates of bite-sized, savory Spanish food designed to be shared around the table. They came over in the early evening, we consulted our cookbooks, headed to the store and then came home to begin chopping, grating, stirring and sautéing for hours on end. Even with the two of us working, it was the longest

I've spent on one meal in all my days in the kitchen. As we worked away over the hot stoves, our spouses hung out in the kitchen with us, drinking wine, telling stories and making fun of our overly meticulous culinary habits. But when we finally made it to the table, it was all worth it.

The meal was incredible. And the conversation was as joyful and hilarious as it was deep and rich. It ranged from parenthood to childhood, from the past to the future, from our most cherished memories to our most fragile dreams. It was indeed a feast, a thin place where we experienced the goodness and nearness of God and glimpsed a little preview of shalom.

As Frederick Buechner has put it, the best moments any of us have as human beings are "those moments when for a little while it is possible to escape the squirrel-cage of being me into the landscape of being us."[9] To share a special meal, lovingly prepared and gratefully enjoyed, with people we care about is one of the greatest means we have of becoming "us." Feasting is a communal practice that binds us together. The table is one of the most powerful places of connection we have as humans. It connects us with our family. It connects us with our friends. And it can connect us with the people who are strangers on the way to becoming friends.

Our dinner tables could be the most "missional" places in all our lives. Perhaps before we invite people to meet Jesus or invite them to church we should invite them to dinner. If feasting is a practice that is vital for shaping and sustaining our life with God for the world, we need to make a point to share our feasts with people who are in our lives but far from God. This was one of the most distinctive aspects of Jesus' ministry. Jesus had a reputation among the religious establishment for being "a glutton and a drunkard." He ate and drank with "notorious sinners." John Dominic Crossan has suggested that Jesus was "the consummate party animal."[10]

When the Pharisees accused him of being "a glutton and a drunkard," they didn't make up that description out of thin air. The phrase comes from Deuteronomy 21, where the Israelites are told what to do with a rebellious son. If a son is stubborn and rebellious and will not respond to his parents' discipline, they are to take him before the elders at the city gate and say, "This son of ours is stubborn and rebellious. He will not obey us. He is a glutton and a drunkard" (Deuteronomy 21:20). The men of the city are then supposed to stone him to death. When the Pharisees call Jesus "a glutton and a drunkard," they are implying that all of his feasting with people who are far from God makes him worthy of death. But for Jesus, it is a demonstration of the inbreaking of the kingdom of God. As Gordon Smith suggests, "Eating was for Jesus a key means by which he proclaimed the coming of God's reign and acted, or enacted, its arrival."[11] And this leads directly to the third aspect of feasting, feasting as an eschatological practice.

Feasting as an eschatological practice. When the prophets wanted to speak of the coming day when God's reign would be uncontested, they depicted a great feast. One of the most evocative expressions of that prophetic imagery is found in Isaiah 25:6-8, where the poet writes about Mt. Zion:

On this mountain the LORD Almighty will prepare
    a feast of rich food for all peoples,
a banquet of aged wine—
    the best of meats and the finest of wines.
On this mountain he will destroy
    the shroud that enfolds all peoples,
    the sheet that covers all nations;
        he will swallow up death forever.
The Sovereign LORD will wipe away the tears
    from all faces;
he will remove his people's disgrace
    from all the earth.
        The LORD has spoken.

Theologian Christine Pohl goes so far as to say, "A shared meal is the activity most closely tied to the reality of God's kingdom, just as it is the most basic expression of hospitality."[12]

In his book *Living Toward a Vision: Biblical Reflections on Shalom*, Walter Brueggemann suggests that we need to learn to see "eating as a shalom event." He goes so far as to say, "If we are to understand shalom at all, I grow more convinced that we shall understand it at the table."[13] A feast filled with joy and vigor, with connection and belonging, is a sign of things to come if we will pay attention. It is a glimpse of the future, of the way things ought to be and the way things one day will be. As Dan Allender writes, "A feast is a rhythm of listening and learning together. A feast is a ritual or remembrance that involves food, music, dancing, and stories; we remember the time when we dined with God in the garden, and we anticipate the day when we will dine with God in the new heavens and earth."[14]

Fasting and the Vision of God

As we seek to shape and sustain our life with God for the world—to live into this story of the already–not yet kingdom—we would do well to recover both the practice of feasting and the practice of fasting. I'll never forget my first experiment in fasting. I was a zealous young college student who had recently stumbled across Richard Foster's contemporary classic *The Celebration of Discipline*. Foster's book opened up for me new understandings of Christian spirituality and new avenues through which to pursue it. After reading his chapter on fasting, I decided to give it a try. Despite his able explanation, I still didn't really know what I was doing. But I picked a day that I thought would be relatively uncomplicated, where I could spend some good time alone with God, and I fasted. My first day of fasting became far more complicated than I had planned when I got called into work. At that time I was working my way through college waiting tables. So I spent the majority of my first day of fasting completely surrounded by food. It seemed the pang in my stomach increased with every plate I served. But I was determined to hold out until the end of my shift and to get away from the food as fast as I could.

When quitting time finally came, I headed back to my apartment feeling tired and cranky, now with an ache in my stomach and a throbbing in my head. Somehow this wasn't feeling very spiritual. Not long after I arrived, my roommate came home earlier than I had expected and asked if I wanted to order a pizza. When I declined, he looked at me puzzled. "Did you already eat?" he asked. When I said I hadn't, he was really perplexed. "Then why don't you want to order a pizza?" I was completely at a loss as to how to reply. The fact of the matter was I did want to order a pizza. There was nothing more I wanted in the world than to order a pizza. But I was fasting. And I was determined to make it. I also remembered Richard Foster making a big deal out of not telling everybody you're fasting and thought I remembered that he'd gotten that from Jesus. I also knew that despite having grown up in the same church, my roommate and I were heading in separate directions spiritually. I knew he'd think I was crazy if I told him I was fasting. So I didn't have a clue how to reply. Finally after stumbling around trying to find an answer, I broke down and told him I was fasting. His response is ever etched in my mind: "Can't you just pray and read your Bible to be spiritual and we can order a pizza?"

"Can't you just pray and read your Bible?" He and I had grown up in the same good evangelical church. We'd been taught that was pretty much the answer to everything. We had been thoroughly trained in a Christianity "from the neck up." But I was going through a season in my life when Christianity from the neck up wasn't doing it for me. I was going through a season of change, loss and confusion, a time when I really needed to know and experience God in ways that "just pray and read your Bible" wasn't addressing. I didn't know it at the time, but I was going through what Scot McKnight has called "a grievous sacred moment." That's why I felt drawn to the practice of fasting. McKnight says, "Fasting is the natural, inevitable response of a person to a grievous sacred moment in life."[15]

Fasting as a defiant practice. Fasting is the way we engage our bodies in our protest against the vandalism of shalom. It is an embodied declaration that things are not the way they're supposed to be. Fasting is a defiant practice—not defiant against God but defiant against the brokenness in our lives and in the world. Sometimes the practice of fasting is presented primarily as a means of developing greater self-control or growing in self-denial. Those good results may in fact be produced in our lives because we choose to fast, but the Bible itself does not present fasting primarily with these ends in view.

In fact, the Bible doesn't really focus on the ends toward which we fast but gives far more attention to the circumstances that evoke the response of fasting from us. Fasting is not primarily a tool to get results. It's a response to the way things are. As McKnight puts it, "The focus in the Christian tradition is not 'if you fast you will get,' but 'when this happens, God's people fast.'"[16] A few examples of reasons God's people fast in the Bible are:

- Loss in battle (Judges 20:26)

- Relief from famine (Jeremiah 14:1-12; Joel 1:14)

- The death of a leader (1 Samuel 31:13; 1 Chronicles 10:12; 2 Samuel 1:12)

- Personal sorrow (1 Samuel 1:7-8; Job 3:24; Psalm 42:1-5)

- The sin of the community (Daniel 9:3-14; Nehemiah 1:4-7)

- Personal sin (2 Samuel 12:16-23; 1 Kings 21:27-29).

Each of these is an example of fasting as a defiant practice, an embodied response to a "grievous sacred moment." Here God's people put their entire selves into their expression to God in the face of a reality that doesn't fit with the way God's world is supposed to be.

Fasting is a way our bodies express the deep longing of our souls in the face of brokenness.

In the opening chapter of the book of Nehemiah, word comes to Nehemiah about the tragic condition of Jerusalem. Nehemiah is eight hundred miles away serving in the palace of a king. He has a comfortable existence. His life is a life of privilege. But when he hears the report that the great city of God is lying in ruin, he is deeply grieved for the holy people and their holy city. Nehemiah learns that Jerusalem, the city of God, is fundamentally broken.

When we encounter the brokenness of our world, we face two very different temptations. First, we can become so overwhelmed that we just want to look away. We would rather continue to walk through life as if nothing was wrong. The problems of the world seem so big we think we're helpless to do anything about them. So we choose to pretend they don't exist.

But there's a second temptation we can face as well. Sometimes we are tempted to dive right in. "I can fix this. I can handle this. I can do something about this." But Nehemiah doesn't give in to either temptation. Nehemiah 1:4 says, "When I heard these things, I sat down and wept. For some days I mourned and fasted and prayed before the God of heaven." Eventually Nehemiah gets up from his knees and engages in a concrete response to the brokenness in his world. But first he looks intently at it and grieves over it. And he fasts. He expresses his heartache and his deep longing for transformation with his body.

There are a lot of things in our lives and in our world that grieve the heart of God and ought to grieve our hearts as well. We must avoid the temptation to look away or the temptation to think naively that we can handle it in our own strength. We need to look intently at reality. To grieve over it. And to fast and pray before the God of heaven. Such fasting is a defiant act—protesting against the vandalism of shalom—that nurtures and sustains life with God for the world.

Fasting as a communal practice. While Jesus clearly warns his followers about fasting in order to be seen by others (Matthew 6:16-18), it's interesting to note that nearly half the references to fasting in the Scriptures refer to corporate fasts—fasting along with other people. There is an important communal dimension to fasting. Sometimes the communal aspect of fasting comes from a community of people who share in a grievous sacred moment. Together they experience brokenness, so together they fast.

In the ancient church, one of the ways the community of faith responded practically to the brokenness they encountered was by fasting. It was one of their concrete responses to the reality of poverty in their midst. Augustine instructed his community,

> First and foremost, clearly, please remember the poor, so that what you withhold from yourselves by living more sparingly, you may deposit in the treasury of heaven. Let the hungry Christ receive what the fasting Christian receives less of. Let the self-denial of one who undertakes it willingly become the support of the one who has nothing. Let the voluntary want of the person who has plenty become the needed plenty of the person in want.[17]

Augustine's words describe a common practice in the early church. Members of the community who had enough fasted on behalf of those who didn't. The food that wasn't eaten by the fasting members of the community was shared with members who were in need. Or the money saved by those who refrained from eating was distributed to those who were poor.

This ancient communal practice of fasting for the poor was a beautiful expression of compassion and a longing for justice. The practice of the early Christians reflected the heart of God captured in Isaiah 58:6-10.

> Is not this the kind of fasting I have chosen:
> to loose the chains of injustice
>   and untie the cords of the yoke,

to set the oppressed free
and break every yoke?
Is it not to share your food with the hungry
and to provide the poor wanderer with shelter—
when you see the naked, to clothe them,
and not to turn away from your own flesh and blood?
Then your light will break forth like the dawn,
and your healing will quickly appear;
then your righteousness will go before you,
and the glory of the LORD will be your rear guard.
Then you will call, and the LORD will answer;
you will cry for help, and he will say: Here am I.
If you do away with the yoke of oppression,
with the pointing finger and malicious talk,
and if you spend yourselves in behalf of the hungry
and satisfy the needs of the oppressed,
then your light will rise in the darkness,
and your night will become like the noonday.

The early church practiced a beautiful form of communal fasting, a fasting for the common good. We would do well in our day to consider the ways we might be able to practice similar forms of fasting. What can we go without in order to provide for others? Can we choose to deny ourselves food for a day so that the money we save can be given to those in need? And what might this look like if we committed to it together as families, as small groups, as missional communities and as churches? In an age of self-indulgence, we need to recover fasting for the common good.

Fasting as an eschatological practice. Finally, we can engage fasting as an eschatological practice, a practice that nurtures our longing for the reign of God to come in its fullness. John Piper writes,

Christian fasting, at its root, is the hunger of a homesickness for

God. . . . Half of Christian fasting is that our physical appetite is lost because our homesickness for God is so intense. The other half is that our homesickness for God is threatened because our physical appetites are so intense. In the first half, appetite is lost. In the second half, appetite is resisted. In the first, we yield to the higher hunger that is. In the second, we fight for the higher hunger that isn't. Christian fasting is not only the spontaneous effect of a superior satisfaction in God; it is also a chosen weapon against every force in the world that would take that satisfaction away.[18]

John the Baptist and his disciples fasted to cultivate this sense of homesickness for God. The great longing of their lives was to see the reign of God show up. Fasting as an eschatological practice can help tap into that hunger, to habituate us to desire the kingdom more than the many other things that compete for our appetites and affections. Fasting feeds our longing for a world set right.

Blessed Are the Placemakers

Living the Vision in
the Contexts of Our Lives

One of the glories of being human
and creaturely is to be implaced.

CRAIG BARTHOLOMEW

The gospel is always conveyed though the medium of culture.
It becomes good news to a lost and broken humanity as it is incarnated
in the world through God's sent people, the church. To be faithful
to its calling, the church must be contextual.

CRAIG VAN GELDER

What the gospel needs most is not intellectual brokers or
cultural diplomats but rather saints who have taken up the way of the cross
and in whose lives the gospel is visible, palpable, and true. It needs disciples
who follow Jesus with or without the support of their culture and
for whom the power of the gospel is demonstrated not
through winning but through obedience.

BRYAN STONE

In his novel *Bleak House,* Charles Dickens includes a chapter called "Telescopic Philanthropy," in which he introduces his readers to a woman named Mrs. Jellyby who operates a boarding house. According to Dickens, Mrs. Jellyby was "a pretty, very diminutive, plump woman of from forty to fifty, with handsome eyes, though they had a curious habit of seeming to look a long way off. As if . . . they could see nothing nearer than Africa!" As Dickens goes on to describe the things and people that make up Mrs. Jellyby's world, he points out signs of neglect. She has an unkempt house, an unkempt husband, unkempt children, unkempt boarders and an unkempt soul. The things that are nearest to her are overlooked and disregarded. As she says in her own words, her attention lies elsewhere. "The African project at present employs my whole time," she says. "It involves me in correspondence with public bodies and with private individuals anxious for the welfare of their species all over the country. I am happy to say it is advancing. We hope by this time next year to have from a hundred and fifty to two hundred healthy families cultivating coffee and educating the natives of Borrioboola-Gha, on the left bank of the Niger."[1]

Dickens's little phrase "telescopic philanthropy" is a remarkably suggestive way to capture the persistent temptation to love our neighbors in the abstract or at a distance. As Christian ethicist Oliver O'Donovan has put it, "To love everybody in the world equally is in fact to love nobody very much."[2] Mrs. Jellyby was so committed to loving her neighbors on the far side of the planet that she failed to love the neighbors she brushed up against every day. Her philanthropy was so telescopic that it failed to see anything or anyone up close.

There is an essential, indissoluble connection between geography and spirituality. We dwell in a particular body at a particular time in a particular place. According to Eugene Peterson,

> In the Christian imagination, where you live gets equal billing with what you believe. Geography and theology are biblical bed-

fellows. Everything that the creator God does, and therefore everything that we do, since we are his creatures and can hardly do anything in any other way, is in place. All living is local—this land, this neighborhood, these trees and streets and houses, this work, these shops and markets.[3]

A spirituality deeply informed by the logic of the incarnation—a life with God for the world—must take seriously the ways we inhabit the particularities of time and place.

Living the Vision in Our Cultural Moment

If "all the world's a stage," as Shakespeare suggested, culture provides the props and the plot in which every human actor plays out his or her role.[4] Like every human being since Adam, Jesus appeared on the scene on a stage that had already been set. When God took on flesh, he took on culture as well. The miracle that stands at the center of the Christian faith—the incarnation of God—happened at a particular time in a particular place, a unique cultural moment. We fundamentally misunderstand the nature of the Christian gospel if we imagine it to be something that floats along above culture as some kind of culture-free, transcendent truth. It is instead the story of God entering the fray of human culture as a culturally situated, culturally conditioned human being.

The challenge of the church in every place and generation throughout its history has been to determine what it means to be faithful to this gospel in the particular cultural environments in which the people of God find themselves. Living out a spirituality deeply informed by the logic of the incarnation necessarily involves learning what it means to be faithful in our time and place, in our unique cultural moment and social location.

The Twilight of Christendom

A number of years ago my wife and I lived in an old house that had been converted into a duplex. We shared the house with two of our dearest friends in a charming little neighborhood filled with Tudor homes built in the 1920s. It was one of the happiest times of our married life. We were expecting our first child. We were sharing life with people we loved. We were making a home and a life for ourselves.

One Tuesday morning as I stood in the living room of that little house ironing my shirt for the day ahead, I watched as a series of baffling events unfolded on the television screen in front of me. I had tuned in to the *Today Show* to fill the quiet in the house as I got ready for work. I watched as the station cut from its scheduled programming to cover what appeared to be an airplane that had crashed into the side of one of the towers of the World Trade Center in New York City. As I continued to watch, I saw a second plane fly into the other tower.

Not knowing what would happen next, but knowing I had a meeting to attend, I headed out the door for work. Along the way I stopped in at Benny's Bagels for a quick breakfast. I stood in Benny's and listened in stunned silence along with the shop attendants and other customers as the radio announcer said that the first tower had collapsed. A few minutes later I arrived at the seminary and gathered with a small group of colleagues crowded around a TV screen and together we watched as the second tower came down.

Undoubtedly, every American conscious of what happened that day could recount a similar tale of their experience when they learned what was going on in New York and Pennsylvania that September morning. The events of 9/11 are forever seared into our personal and national consciousness. To this day, every time I walk into that bagel shop, the sights and smells immediately take me back to that day.

September 11, 2001, is the closest thing in recent American history that comes anywhere near the experience of confusion, fear and dislocation felt by the ancient people of God when Jerusalem was attacked and demolished by the Babylonians. In 586 B.C., Nebuchadnezzar II, the king of Babylon—the despotic terrorist of the ancient Fertile Crescent—

besieged the city of Jerusalem. He came with his armies, tore down the walls, decimated the city, looted the houses and left the temple in a pile of rubble. The holy of holies, believed by the people of Israel to be the dwelling place of God on earth, became ground zero.

Nebuchadnezzar II carried the riches of the temple back to Babylon and took with him several thousand Jews, bringing them into exile to try to undo all they had learned about what it meant to be God's people and making them good Babylonians. He sought to give them an altogether new identity so that never again would they rise up and stand against the king and his power.

According to Walter Brueggemann, "The exiles experienced a loss of the structured, reliable world which gave them meaning and coherence, and they found themselves in a context where their most treasured and trusted symbols of faith were mocked, trivialized, or dismissed."[5] As Brueggemann and others have pointed out, the experience of the church in North America today mirrors Israel's experience in exile in some important ways. For centuries the church in the Western world experienced an unparalleled power, privilege and prestige in society. This condition, known as "Christendom," stretches all the way back to the time of Constantine, the fourth-century Roman emperor.

In A.D. 313 Constantine issued the Edict of Milan, which made Christianity a legal religion within the Roman Empire. In a short period of time Christianity went from being a legal religion to being *the* legal religion. Before Constantine it was socially disadvantageous to be a Christian. After Constantine it became socially disadvantageous not to be a Christian. And from that time forward, everything changed for the church. In Christendom, church and culture became deeply intertwined. Christians felt at home in a cultural environment that reinforced their most cherished convictions, provided them numerous social advantages and passed along Christian values and morality as part of the basic social inheritance.

But all of that has profoundly changed. The ground has shifted under our feet. As Bryan Stone writes, "The church can no longer assume as it once did that the surrounding culture will assist in the task of producing Christians. The home base from which Christians thought to Christianize the rest of the world feels less and less like 'home,' despite the desperate attempts by some to keep it that way."[6] Many among us might pine for the good old days. But nostalgia is unlikely to get us very far. Instead we need to learn from the experience of Israel in exile as we seek to live faithfully in the time and place to which God has called us. As we do, we may discover that the demise of Christendom is less a death to lament than an opportunity to embrace. As Stone writes,

> Ironically, it may be that it is precisely from a position of marginality that the church is best able to announce peace and to bear witness to God's peaceable reign in such a way as to invite others to take seriously the subversive implications of that reign. It may be that through humility, repentance, and disavowal of its former advantages, so that those things which once were "gains" the church now comes to regard as "loss" (Phil 3:7), a church at the periphery of the world may yet be a church for the world.[7]

The people of God in exile could have easily been seduced by an illusion of what faithfulness looked like in Babylon. They could have held on to a false belief that all they needed to do was hunker down and wait, keep themselves isolated from and uncorrupted by their host culture. In fact, false prophets were promoting this isolationist agenda by declaring that God would soon deliver his people from the hands of the Babylonians and return them to their homeland. Not surprisingly, this was an attractive lie that sounded pious and convinced many that faithfulness meant patient endurance in isolation until the day they would all go home.

To be sure, there are many Christians in our contemporary exilic condition for whom the isolationist option seems good and right. Like the people of Israel in Babylon, they see just how corrupt the host culture is and they don't want to be corrupted by it. Instead they construct Christian alternatives to the structures of the broader society. Buoyed by the hope that one day they'll be evacuated from this place that's destined for destruction, they're convinced that "this world is not my home; I'm just a passing through. . . . And I can't feel at home in this world anymore."

Another option available in our day that was unavailable to the Old Testament exilic community is the posture of the "culture warrior." Rather than adopt a position of isolation, these Christians are eager to reclaim lost ground. These Christians are quick to decry the moral decay of much of contemporary American culture and are intent on reversing these devastating trends. Nostalgic for the way things once were, Christians who adopt the "culture war" mentality and rhetoric usually display a strong sense of confidence in the prospects of conservative politics to undo what's been done.

A third possibility presented by our contemporary exilic condition that was a danger to the ancient exiles as well is the potential of assimilation. Certainly the intention of Nebuchadnezzar was to form the Israelites into good Babylonians. He wanted their immersion in the host culture to strip them of anything distinctively Jewish. Something similar can happen to Christians in North America today. In our efforts to fit in with the broader culture or to be relevant to the broader culture, we can unwittingly become so much like that culture that we fail to embody a way of life that's in any way distinctively Christian.

None of these options fits with what faithfulness looked like for the exiles of the Old Testament. Instead they received instructions from the prophet Jeremiah regarding how they were to pursue faithfulness in Babylon. In Jeremiah 29:4-7 the prophet writes,

> This is what the LORD Almighty, the God of Israel, says to all those
> I carried into exile from Jerusalem to Babylon: "Build houses and
> settle down; plant gardens and eat what they produce. Marry and
> have sons and daughters; find wives for your sons and give your
> daughters in marriage, so that they too may have sons and daughters.
> Increase in number there; do not decrease. Also, seek the peace and
> prosperity of the city to which I have carried you into exile. Pray to
> the LORD for it, because if it prospers, you too will prosper."

Yahweh's instruction through his prophet was literally for his people
to "seek the shalom of the city . . . for in its shalom is your shalom." The
exiles were instructed to pursue the dream of God for the city, to seek
the shalom of Babylon. Again Brueggemann's comments are helpful:
"There is no 'separate peace' for exiles, no private deals with God, no
permitted withdrawal from the affairs of the empire. The only shalom
these troubled Jews would know is the shalom wrought for Babylon."

God's people would flourish in the place of their exile by actively
promoting the flourishing of their neighbors and enemies. This would
require of them on the one hand to maintain their distinctive identity
as the people of God. But on the other hand it would require them to
become active participants in the host culture. Brueggemann continues, "The letter implies that the exiled community of Jews can
indeed impact Babylon with shalom through its active concern and
prayer, but only as the community knows that it is not Babylon. The
distance from Babylon makes possible an impacting nearness to
Babylon."[9] The Old Testament exiles were instructed to become active
cultural agents in the place God had put them, "placemakers" who
built houses, planted gardens, thrived as families and contributed to
the well-being of their neighbors.

Question-Posing Lives

In the New Testament, the apostle Peter used the metaphor of exile to address the situation of a group of Christians who were seeking to be faithful in their time and place in a very inhospitable cultural environment. In 1 Peter 2:11-12 he wrote, "Dear friends, I urge you, as foreigners and exiles, to abstain from sinful desires, which wage war against your soul. Live such good lives among the pagans that, though they — accuse you of doing wrong, they may see your good deeds and glorify God on the day he visits us." Peter's words echo those of Jesus from the Sermon on the Mount: "Let your light shine before others, that they may see your good deeds and glorify your Father in heaven" (Matthew 5:16). Peter says this must be the posture of the Christian community even (perhaps especially) in the midst of a hostile cultural environment.

A little further on, as Peter spells out what it means to live good lives among the pagans, he writes,

> Who is going to harm you if you are eager to do good? But even if you should suffer for what is right, you are blessed. "Do not fear their threats; do not be frightened." But in your hearts revere Christ as Lord. Always be prepared to give an answer to everyone who asks you to give the reason for the hope that you have. But do this with gentleness and respect, keeping a clear conscience, so that those who speak maliciously against your good behavior in Christ may be ashamed of their slander. (1 Peter 3:13-16)

Peter's instructions here are suggestive of the kind of life the Christian community is called to live in exile. His admonition assumes that people will ask questions about the hope we have. He assumes we will live question-posing lives in the view of our neighbors. He instructs his hearers to live good lives—lives of integrity, compassion and justice—"among the pagans," in such a way that those lives are noticed. We are not to be isolated from the culture but integrated into its fabric. And the assumption is that when we live that kind of life, people will be provoked to ask about the hope we've found. There are two contexts we need to rediscover if we're going to live question-posing lives

in the view of our neighbors: the context of the parish and the context
of the neighborhood.

Rediscovering the parish. For many modern churches, location is
a somewhat arbitrary issue. In the Dallas metro area where I live, it is
not at all uncommon for me to encounter people who commute
twenty or thirty minutes to the church they attend. I've even known
folks who have driven an hour to continue to be part of a church they
had moved away from. Even when the commute to church is not so
extreme, people often find themselves connecting with other church
members who live an equal distance to the church but in the opposite
direction. We've created church structures that make it easy for us to
worship in a place that's far from home and to "do life" with people in
places even farther removed. Such an approach to church life not only
makes genuine *koinonia* with other members virtually impossible; it
also militates against living the kind of question-posing lives in the
view of our neighbors described by the apostle Peter. One great need
of churches in our day is the rediscovery of the concept of parish.

While the term *parish* is still employed today in Roman Catholic
and Anglican circles, for most evangelical church leaders it's something of a foreign concept. Understood in its most basic sense, a parish
is a local church with a distinctive emphasis on the word *local.* The
word *parish* is etymologically connected to two Greek words, *para*
and *oikos*. *Para* means "by" or "near" and *oikos* means "house." This
etymology points to the distinctively local meaning of parish. The
word points to both the "church near the house" and the "houses near
the church." In Catholic and Anglican ecclesial structures, the parish
is the smallest, most local expression of church. The parish is a local
church living in and for a place. A parish is a community of people in
a specific geographical location taking holistic responsibility for that
place. As such, the word *parish* can be used to refer both to the church
itself and to the surrounding community of which it is a part.

Both members and leaders of parish-minded churches take on a kind of holistic responsibility for the people who live in proximity to the church, whether they are participants in the church or not. A parish-minded church doesn't just provide religious goods and services within a particular geographic community; it is invested in the flourishing of that community. It shares its burdens. It knows its broken places. It pursues the dream of God for the particular place to which it has been called. While it may invest resources in the mission of God in faraway places, it invests itself—its communal, embodied life—in the mission of God at a profoundly local level.

Perhaps the most fundamental posture of a parish-minded church is the posture of listening. When Jesus encountered Bartimaeus, the blind man on the road to Jericho, he asked him, "What do you want me to do for you?" (Mark 10:51). This is the fundamental question of the parish-minded church. The parish-minded church asks the people of its geographic community about their deepest needs, longings and aspirations for the place they live and the people who live there. The church that seeks to rediscover significance of "parish" must identify its unique parish predicament. What are the unique needs and opportunities of the place to which God has called us? How can we live good lives and bring good news in particular ways suited to these particular people in this particular place? A parish-minded church is attentive and responsive to the unique needs of the place where God has put it.

The church that seeks to rediscover the significance of "parish" must also uncover its unique parish potential. What is God already up to in this place and with these people? Where are there signs of life and flourishing that we can join? What unique resources do we have to contribute to the good of our parish? How can we bring those resources to bear in response to our parish predicament?

Irving Bible Church, the church I serve as a teaching pastor, existed for years as a fairly typical suburban megachurch. Our worship was captivating, our teaching was inspiring and our programs were rel-

evant to people's everyday lives. We followed many of the typical
church growth strategies and experienced a rapid rate of growth. But
at some point in our journey our leaders began to wrestle with our
sense of identity and calling, our sense of what it meant to be the
church. And we began to rediscover the meaning of the parish, to take
holistic responsibility for the people in the place that God had put us.
We began to ask what the greatest needs were in our parish and how
we were uniquely resourced to meet those needs.

There is a remarkable economic and ethnic diversity in close proximity to our church. In the immediate vicinity to the north of our
campus you'll find a lot of new development filled with affluent, upper-
middle-class families. But to the south of our campus you'll find an
older community made up of families who face significantly greater
economic hardship, many of whom are newcomers to the country. We
began to look for the connections between our parish predicament
and our parish potential.

As a result we have developed things like our health clinic, where
we use our facility as a place where medical professionals and a host
of caring volunteers from our congregation provide free health care
to some of the underresourced people in our parish. We have volunteers who teach English as a second language and who lead citizenship
classes. We have a strong partnership with the Irving Independent
School District and provide "reading buddies" and lunchtime mentors
for kids in our local elementary and middle schools. We partner with
an organization called Family Promise to use our facility as temporary
housing for homeless families from our parish and to help them gain
the skills they need to get back on their feet. We've developed a strong
relationship with our local municipal government, which now often
comes to us when there is a problem in our community that needs to
be addressed. All of this has happened because our suburban megachurch began to rediscover what it meant to be a parish church and
began to ask how we could connect the potential of our people with

the predicament of our place.

Rediscovering the neighborhood. If we are going to live question-posing lives in the view of our neighbors, we not only need churches that rediscover the context of the parish; we need Christians who rediscover the context of the neighborhood. We need to think of the places we live and the people who live there as our own "personal parish," the place God has planted us and the people he's called us to love. The neighbors who live in closest proximity to us are usually not people we've chosen, but they are "those who have been given to us" and "those to whom we have been given."[10]

Of course, our contemporary life patterns often don't lend themselves to being good neighbors. We're a culture largely defined by the automobile and we spend more and more time in our cars. Our commutes get longer and longer as our suburbs continue to expand farther and farther from our city centers. According to Albert Hsu, the amount of time the average American now spends commuting, if consolidated, would be over three weeks a year.[11]

And the modern neighborhood isn't designed in a way that fosters neighborliness. At the end of our long commutes, many of us drive into our driveway, put up the automatic garage door, close it behind us, and enter into our climate-controlled havens without ever even having had the chance to see our neighbors. Many of our newer neighborhoods don't have sidewalks for people to walk on, front porches for people to sit and talk on, or any public-use spaces for people to gather in. Some of us live such busy lives that we hire people to work in our yards for us and we're on the go so much we do little more in our homes than sleep.

These realities present serious spiritual problems. Our constant busyness and our fragmented lifestyles are toxic to the soul. And such patterns of life make it virtually impossible to live question-posing lives in the view of our neighbors. People don't ask us to give the reason for our hope because they can't see it impacting our day-to-day lives. They can't even *see* our day-to-day lives.

One of the most important biblical commands we need to hear in the midst of our busyness and fragmentation is the simple command from the apostle Paul in Romans 12:13: "Practice hospitality." The word Paul uses here literally means "love a stranger." That sounds like a frightening concept to many of us, as it seems to imply taking a random person off of the street into our home. But for many of us, the people in are neighborhoods are in fact strangers to us.

Christine Pohl describes the importance of practicing hospitality in the life of the early church when she writes, "Hospitality to needy strangers distinguished the early church from its surrounding environment. Noted as exceptional by Christians and non-Christians alike, offering care to strangers became one of the distinguishing marks of the authenticity of the Christian gospel and of the church."[12] Their acts of hospitality were grounded in the hospitality of God, and their demonstrable love toward their neighbors became one of the most significant factors in the spread of the gospel throughout the Roman Empire. And their context bears a significant resemblance to our own. Pohl continues,

> Our contemporary situation is surprisingly similar to the early Christian context in which the normative understanding and practices of hospitality were developed. We, like the early church, find ourselves in a fragmented and multicultural society that yearns for relationships, identity, and meaning. Our mobile and self-oriented society is characterized by disturbing levels of loneliness, alienation, and estrangement. . . . People are hungry for welcome but most Christians have lost track of the heritage of hospitality.[13]

People in our neighborhoods are indeed "hungry for welcome." If we truly want to live life with God for the world, we must rethink how we relate to the world, which means rethinking how we relate to the world closest to us—rethinking how we relate to our neighbors. Here are a handful of relatively simple but imminently practical ways for us to pursue connections with the people in our neighborhoods:

- *Stay home.* We can't possibly be good neighbors if we're never home. Often we work outside the neighborhood, worship outside the neighborhood, shop outside the neighborhood, eat outside the neighborhood and play outside the neighborhood. And much of this is unavoidable. But we need to examine the choices we make and look for ways we can prioritize being more fully present in our personal parish.

- *Go outside.* We miss opportunities for spontaneous interaction with our neighbors because we're not outside at the same time. The only way to counteract that reality is to spend more time outside. Sit on the front porch. Play in the front yard. Take regular walks around the neighborhood.

- *Pay attention.* We're often so busy or so distracted that we fail to notice what's going on right around us. We often fail to even see our neighbors. Without becoming invasive, we need to learn to be better about observing what's happing in the lives of people around us.

- *Celebrate.* One of the best ways to make connections with people in our neighborhood is to throw a party. Look for opportunities for celebration and be intentional about including the people around you. Jesus knew how to throw a good dinner party. So should his followers.

- *Ask questions.* We get to know people by getting to know their stories. We get to know their stories by asking them questions. Look for opportunities to ask your neighbors about their lives.

- *Pray.* While it might seem cliché, praying for our neighbors regularly is a remarkably important way to invest in our neighborhood. We tend to care more for and pay more attention to the things we pray about regularly.

- *Show up.* Whether it's a cup of sugar, a ride to the airport or something more substantial, good neighbors have opportunities to help one another in times of need. Don't miss those opportunities when they present themselves. (And it doesn't hurt to borrow a cup of sugar from them from time to time, too.)

As we make connections with our neighbors, we have the opportunity to see them move from being strangers to becoming friends. This happens best when we invite them to our table. The dinner table may very well be the most missional place in all our lives. More and more churches are transitioning their traditional small group programs to "family dinner" groups. Rather than sitting in a closed circle discussing the Bible, they sit at an open table and live the Bible by experiencing *koinonia* and inviting neighbors to "taste and see" the beauty of Christian community.

Moving In

Not long ago my family moved into a new neighborhood. Our goal was to make life smaller, to live closer to where I work and where we worship so that our lives would be more integrated, less complicated. When you're in the market for a new home, a real estate agent will tell you that there are three considerations that are fundamentally important: location, location, location. I've become convinced that the same thing is true when it comes to spirituality and mission. When it comes to living life with God for the world, there are three considerations that are fundamentally important: location, location, location. In his classic paraphrase of the book of John, Eugene Peterson writes, "And the Word became flesh and blood and moved into the neighborhood" (John 1:14, *The Message*). Incarnation was divine implacement. A spirituality deeply informed by the logic of the incarnation is a spirituality of implacement. We dwell in a particular body at a particular time in a particular place. One of the main ways that our Babylon wants to press us into its mold is to see us live its frenetic, fragmented way of life. But we must learn from the ancient people of God in their condition of exile as we figure out how to live as foreigners and exiles in our own day. God's word to them is God's word to us. Blessed are the placemakers. "Seek the shalom of the city to which I have carried you . . . for in its shalom is your shalom."

Conclusion

*Sometimes the desire to save the
whole world can be an impediment to taking
even one small action to improve it.*

George Prochnik

*We have been called to heal wounds,
to unite what has fallen apart, and to bring
home those who have lost their way.*

St. Francis of Assisi

*It's only by journeying for the world's sake,
even when it sickens and scares you to death,
that little by little we start to come alive.*

Frederick Buechner

I've discovered that writing a book about spirituality and mission is a great way to reveal just how far short you fall of your own highest ideals. Throughout the process of writing this book my prayer has been, "Lord, help me not to write better than I live." But a grand vision of life with God for the world is a hard thing to live up to. In reality, we often live our lives fairly oblivious to God and almost exclusively for ourselves. Our own best aspirations can be difficult to achieve.

The 2008 movie *Brideshead Revisited* is a film adaptation of the novel written by Evelyn Waugh, a British novelist of the first half of the twentieth century. Waugh was well known for his outspoken commitment to his Christian faith and also for being completely impossible to get along with. He was once criticized by his fellow author, Nancy Mitford, for the apparent contradiction between his ostentatious religious commitment and his personal nastiness. Upon hearing Mitford's complaint, Waugh famously replied, "You have no idea how horrible I would be if I were not a Christian." Waugh's retort says something true of all of us. We're not the Christians we ought to be. But we're better off with Jesus than we would be on our own.

I remember sitting in a coffee shop in Wheaton, Illinois, a few years ago. It was a cold winter day, and I was watching the snow fall outside the big window next to my table. I was thinking about the fact that it had been twenty years since I had become a Christian. As I sat there, one particular thought rolled around in my head. I thought, "God, it's been twenty years. I thought you would have fixed me by now." I take great comfort in the words of the fourteenth-century devotional writer Julian of Norwich: "Our courteous Lord does not want his servants to despair even if they fall frequently and grievously. Our falling does not stop his loving us." Those of us who aspire to become missional Christians need the regular reminder that our acceptance with God has nothing to do with our performance for him.

I'm also comforted to know that, by his own admission, one of the great missional Christians of the church's history, the apostle Paul, was a man marked by weakness. I find his honesty about his own sin and suffering to be remarkable when compared to the surrounding world at the time. In Paul's day there was an incredibly high value placed on maintaining honor. To show your weakness, to let others see your vulnerability, was to bring shame on yourself. In that culture few things were more important than honor and few things worse than shame. The Stoic philosopher Plutarch once sent a letter to his wife called "On Consolation on the Death of a Child" in which he essentially said to her, "Get over it. It was just a child. The more important thing is my reputation as a moral philosopher. And your excessive grieving brings me into ill repute. So go off and grieve quietly if you need to, but be sure that you do all you can to maintain my reputation."[1] Elsewhere, Plutarch claimed that the sage of the Stoics "is not impeded when confined and under no compulsion when flung down a precipice and not in torture when on the rack and not injured when mutilated . . . and is uncaptured while his enemies are selling him into slavery."[2]

It's fascinating to compare this to the apostle Paul, who called himself the "the worst" of sinners (1 Timothy 1:15). In 2 Corinthians 12:7-10, Paul writes straightforwardly about his weakness:

> Therefore, in order to keep me from becoming conceited, I was given a thorn in my flesh, a messenger of Satan, to torment me. Three times I pleaded with the Lord to take it away from me. But he said to me, "My grace is sufficient for you, for my power is made perfect in weakness." Therefore I will boast all the more gladly about my weaknesses, so that Christ's power may rest on me. That is why, for Christ's sake, I delight in weaknesses, in insults, in hardships, in persecutions, in difficulties. For when I am weak, then I am strong.

I'm becoming more and more convinced that the profoundly missional character of Paul's life—his life with God for the world—did not evidence itself in spite of his weakness but through it. His deep sense of his own need drove him to God's grace. And his deep gratitude for that grace compelled him toward mission. Paul's keen awareness of his own weakness helped him never get over the beauty of the gospel, helped him never cease to be stunned by the reality that Christ took on our weakness in his incarnation in order to bring us life and to show us how to live fully human lives.

Life with God for the world is the life we were made for, the life Jesus came to secure and the life we now wait for in hope. That hope breaks in on our lives now, transforming our hearts and our patterns of living as we experience the nearness of God's presence through the Spirit, as we live into the just reign Jesus came to begin, and as we grasp glimpses of the perfect peace of the world to come in the midst of the world as we know it. To live into this vision is to flourish as the kind of beings God has made us to be. It is to learn to live fully human lives after the pattern of the one who was fully human and fully God. This is life. Real life. Abundant life. Life of the age to come lived here and now. And so I conclude with a fitting plea from a fourth-century liturgical prayer from Serapion of Thmuis:

Lord, we beg you, make us truly alive.

Notes

Introduction: The Incarnation and Christian Spirituality

[1]Jacques Ellul, *The Presence of the Kingdom*, 2nd ed., trans. Olive Wyon (Colorado Springs: Helmers and Howard, 1989), p. 120.

[2]See "'Nones' on the Rise," Pew Research Religion and Public Life Project, October 9, 2012, www.pewforum.org/2012/10/09/nones-on-the-rise.

[3]See David Kinnaman, *You Lost Me: Why Young Christians Are Leaving the Church . . . and Rethinking Faith* (Grand Rapids: Baker Books, 2011).

[4]Gabe Lyons, *The Next Christians: The Good News About the End of Christian America* (New York: Doubleday Religion, 2010), p. 11.

[5]Eugene Peterson, *Subversive Spirituality* (Grand Rapids: Eerdmans, 1997), p. 8.

[6]Ibid., p. 6.

[7]David Augsburger, *Dissident Discipleship: A Spirituality of Self-Surrender, Love of God, and Love of Neighbor* (Grand Rapids: Brazos, 2006), p. 10.

[8]Jean Twenge and Keith Campbell, *The Narcissism Epidemic: Living in the Age of Entitlement* (New York: Free Press, 2009), p. 31.

[9]Ibid.

[10]Ibid., p. 4.

[11]Philip Rieff, *The Triumph of the Therapeutic: Uses of Faith After Freud* (San Francisco: Harper & Row, 1966).

[12]Christopher Lasch, *The Culture of Narcissism: American Life in an Age of Diminishing Expectations* (New York: W. W. Norton, 1979), p. 7.

[13]Peterson, *Subversive Spirituality*, p. 15.

[14]David Gushee, "Spiritual Formation and the Sanctity of Life," in *Life in the Spirit: Spiritual Formation in Theological Perspective*, ed. Jeffrey Greenman and George Kalantzis (Downers Grove, IL: InterVarsity Press, 2010), p. 213.

[15]Gordon MacDonald, "The Danger of Missionalism," *Leadership Journal*, January 1, 2007.

[16]Anthony Bradley, "The 'New Legalism,'" *World*, May 4, 2013, www.worldmag .com/2013/05/the_new_legalism.

[17]See the discussion in Darrell Guder, ed., *The Missional Church: A Vision for the Sending of the Church in North America* (Grand Rapids: Eerdmans, 1998), p. 93.

[18]James K. A. Smith, *Desiring the Kingdom: Worship, Worldview and Cultural Formation* (Grand Rapids: Baker Academic, 2009), p. 53.

[19]Craig Dykstra, *Growing in the Life of Faith: Education and Christian Practices*, 2nd ed. (Louisville, KY: Westminster John Knox, 2005), p. 48, n. 16.

[20]John R. W. Stott, *The Message of Ephesians*, The Bible Speaks Today (Downers Grove, IL: InterVarsity Press, 1986), p. 193.

[21]David Bosch, *A Spirituality of the Road* (Eugene, OR: Wipf and Stock, 2001), p. 12.

[22]Irenaeus, *Adversus Haereses*, 4.20.

Chapter 1: The Stories We Live and the Stories We Live Into

[1]Walter Hooper, ed., *They Stand Together: The Letters of C. S. Lewis to Arthur Greeves* (New York: Macmillan, 1979), p. 425. I'm grateful for Kurt Bruner for drawing my attention to this important conversation between Lewis and Tolkien. See his lecture "Finding God in the *Lord of the Rings*," available at www.kurtbrunner.com.

[2]Gregory Mobley, *The Return of the Chaos Monster—And Other Biblical Backstories* (Grand Rapids: Eerdmans, 2012), p. 6.

[3]James K. A. Smith, *Who's Afraid of Postmodernism: Taking Derrida, Lyotard, and Foucault to Church* (Grand Rapids: Baker Academic, 2006), p. 144.

[4]Eugene Peterson, *Eat This Book: A Conversation in the Art of Spiritual Reading* (Grand Rapids: Eerdmans, 2009), pp. 43-44.

[5]Gabriel Fackre, *The Christian Story* (Grand Rapids: Eerdmans, 1978), p. 31.

[6]Richard J. Foster with Kathryn A. Helmers, *Life with God: Reading the Bible for Spiritual Transformation* (San Francisco: HarperOne, 2008), p. 7.

[7]This is a favorite phrase of Tom Wright to describe the relationship between heaven and earth. See his *Simply Christian: Why Christianity Makes Sense* (San Francisco: HarperSanFrancisco, 2006), pp. 63-66.

[8]Walter Brueggemann, *Living Toward a Vision: Biblical Reflections on Shalom* (New York: United Church Press, 1976), p. 16.

[9]This phrase comes from Cornelius Plantinga's brilliant account of sin, *Not the Way It's Supposed to Be: A Breviary of Sin* (Grand Rapids: Eerdmans, 1995).

[10]Dietrich Bonhoeffer, *Creation and Fall/Temptation*, trans. John C. Fletcher (New York: Simon and Schuster, 1997), p. 9.

[11]The apostle Peter also picks up Isaiah's language when he writes, "But in keeping with his promise we are looking forward to a new heaven and a new earth, where righteousness dwells" (2 Peter 3:13).

[12]See T. Desmond Alexander, *From Eden to the New Jerusalem: An Introduction to Biblical Theology* (Grand Rapids: Kregel, 2008), p. 59. Alexander lists seventy-four different passages that speak of a radically transformed Jerusalem: forty-three in Isaiah, thirteen in Jeremiah, ten in Ezekiel and eight in Zechariah.

[13]Among the many connections to which they point is the shape of this great city coming down out of heaven. According to John, the New Jerusalem is "as wide and high as it is long" (Revelation 21:16). This great world-encompassing city is a perfect cube. The natural question to ask when we encounter such an obscure detail, particularly in the book of Revelation, is "where have we seen this before?" There is only one other place in the Bible that depicts a perfect cube like this one. In 1 Kings 6, the author describes the construction of the temple in Jerusalem: "The inner sanctuary was twenty cubits long, twenty wide and twenty high" (1 Kings 6:20). Besides the New Jerusalem, the only other cube mentioned in the Bible is the inner sanctuary of the Jerusalem temple—the holy of holies—the place Jewish tradition claimed as the dwelling place of God.

[14]Gordon Wenham, quoted in Alexander, *From Eden*, p. 21.

[15]G. K. Beale, *The Temple and the Church's Mission: A Biblical Theology of the Dwelling Place of God*, New Studies in Biblical Theology (Downers Grove, IL: InterVarsity Press, 2004), p. 369. Beale spells out fourteen distinct lines of evidence in support of his contention that the garden of Eden should be understood as "the first archetypal temple in which the first man worshiped God" (p. 66). See especially pp. 66-80.

[16]This image of a river flowing from the heart of the city further reinforces our understanding of the New Jerusalem as a city-temple. The prophet Ezekiel told of a day when a life-giving river would flow from the restored temple (Ezekiel 47:1-12).

[17]Enrique Nardoni, *Rise Up, O Judge: A Study of Justice in the Biblical World*, trans. Seán Charles Martin (Peabody, MA: Hendrickson, 2004), p. 318.

[18]Bonhoeffer, *Creation and Fall*, p. 51.

[19]Nicholas Wolterstorff, *Until Justice and Peace Embrace* (Grand Rapids: Eerdmans, 1983), p. 69.

[20]Helmut Thielicke, *How the World Began: Man in the First Chapters of the Bible*, trans. John W. Doberstein (Philadelphia: Muhlenberg, 1961), pp. 103, 106.

[21]Ibid., p. 103.

[22]I owe this insight to the teaching of Rikk Watts. See his lecture series *It's About Life: A Biblical Journey*, Regent College, March 18, 2011, MP3 audio, available at www.regentaudio.com/products/its-about-life-a-biblical -journey.

[23]Herman Bavinck, quoted in by Donald Bloesch, *Spirituality Old and New: Recovering Authentic Spiritual Life* (Downers Grove, IL: IVP Academic, 2007), p. 77.

[24]Lesslie Newbigin, *Foolishness to the Greeks: The Gospel and Western Culture* (Grand Rapids: Eerdmans, 1986), p. 133.

[25]Wright, *Simply Christian*, p. 236.

[26]Fackre, *Christian Story*, p. 99.

Chapter 2: Bent and Broken

[1]Blaise Pascal, *Christianity for Modern Pagans: Pascal's Pensées Edited, Outlined, and Explained*, ed. Peter Kreeft, trans. A. J. Krailsheimer (San Francisco: Ignatius, 1993), p. 65.

[2]Cornelius Plantinga, *Not the Way It's Supposed to Be: A Breviary of Sin* (Grand Rapids: Eerdmans, 1995), p. ix.

[3]Richard Rohr, "Discerning Our Complicity," February 28, 2012, from Richard's Daily Meditations, available through the Center for Action and Contemplation, https://cac.org/richard-rohr/daily-meditations.

[4]The "Great Rupture" is Jacques Ellul's preferred phrase to refer to what is commonly called "the Fall." See his *The Humiliation of the Word* (Grand Rapids: Eerdmans, 1985), chapter 7.

[5]Peter Kreeft, "C. S. Lewis's Argument from Desire," in *The Riddle of Joy: G. K. Chesterton and C. S. Lewis*, ed. Michael MacDonald and Andrew Tadie (San Francisco: HarperCollins, 1989), p. 260.

[6]T. Desmond Alexander, *From Eden to the New Jerusalem: An Introduction to Biblical Theology* (Grand Rapids: Kregel, 2008), pp. 78-79.

[7]Plantinga, *Not the Way*, p. 14.

[8]Ibid., p. 26.

[9]Walter Brueggemann, *Living Toward a Vision: Biblical Reflections on Shalom* (New York: United Church Press, 1976), p. 148.

[10]Lesslie Newbigin, *The Good Shepherd: Meditations on Christian Ministry in Today's World* (Grand Rapids: Eerdmans, 1977), p. 96.

[11]David Bosch, *Spirituality of the Road* (Eugene, OR: Wipf and Stock, 2001), p. 15.

[12]Newbigin, *Good Shepherd*, p. 98.

[13]Rodney Clapp, *Tortured Wonders: Christian Spirituality for People, Not Angels* (Grand Rapids: Brazos, 2004), pp. 36, 38.

[14]Scot McKnight, *Galatians*, NIV Application Commentary (Grand Rapids: Zondervan, 1995), p. 266.

[15]See Anthony C. Thiselton, "Flesh," in *New International Dictionary of New Testament Theology*, vol. 1, ed. Colin Brown (Grand Rapids: Zondervan, 1986), p. 680.

[16]See Matt Jenson, *The Gravity of Sin: Augustine, Luther and Barth on 'homo incurvatus in se'* (London: T & T Clark, 2007).

[17]Gabriel Fackre, *The Christian Story* (Grand Rapids: Eerdmans, 1978), p. 72.

[18]C. S. Lewis, *The Screwtape Letters* (New York: HarperCollins, 2001), p. 44.

[19]See Brené Brown's TED talk, "The Power of Vulnerability," TEDxHouston, June 2010, www.ted.com/talks/brene_brown_on_vulnerability.html.

[20]Frederick Buechner, *The Clown in the Belfry: Writings on Faith and Fiction* (New York: HarperCollins, 1992), pp. 98-99.

[21]Michael Mangis, *Signature Sins: Taming Our Wayward Hearts* (Downers Grove, IL: InterVarsity Press, 2008), p. 145.

[22]Dan Allender, *The Healing Path: How the Hurts in Your Past Can Lead to a More Abundant Life* (Colorado Springs: WaterBrook, 1999), p. 85.

[23]Newbigin, *Good Shepherd*, p. 99.

Chapter 3: The Dwelling Place of God

[1]See Frederick Dale Bruner and William Horden, *The Holy Spirit: Shy Member of the Trinity* (Eugene, OR: Wipf and Stock, 2001).

[2]Gordon Fee, *Paul, The Spirit, and the People of God* (Peabody, MA: Hendrickson, 1996), p. 22.

[3]This is a traditional Jewish prayer known as Tefilat Geshem, available at http://lpjc.org/teffilat-geshemmashiv-haruach.

[4]John Calvin, *Institutes of the Christian Religion*, 1.6.8.

[5]N. T. Wright, *Simply Christian: Why Christianity Makes Sense* (San Francisco: HarperOne, 2006), p. 124.

[6]Calvin, *Institutes*, 3.2.7.

[7]Calvin, *Institutes*, 3.2.17.

[8]Ibid.

[9]Wright, *Simply Christian*, p. 122.

[10]Michael Frost, *The Road to Missional: Journey to the Center of the Church* (Grand Rapids: Baker Books, 2011), p. 28.

[11]Ibid.

[12]John Zizioulas, "The Early Christian Community," in *Christian Spirituality: Origins to the Twelfth Century*, World Spirituality 16 (New York: Crossroads, 1987), p. 27.

[13]Rodney Clapp, *Tortured Wonders: Christian Spirituality for People, Not Angels* (Grand Rapids: Brazos, 2004), p. 18.

[14]J. I. Packer, *Keeping in Step with the Spirit: Finding Fullness in Our Walk with God* (Grand Rapids: Baker Books, 1984), p. 57, emphasis original.

Chapter 4: Glimpses of the World to Come

[1]Søren Kierkegaard, "The Practice in Christianity," in *The Essential Kierkegaard*, ed. Howard V. Hong and Edna H. Hong (Princeton, NJ: Princeton University Press, 2000), p. 381.

[2]Frederick Buechner, *Wishful Thinking: A Seeker's ABC* (San Francisco: HarperSanFrancisco, 1993), p. 18.

[3]James D. G. Dunn, *Jesus' Call to Discipleship* (Cambridge: Cambridge University Press, 1992), p. 73.

[4]N. T. Wright, *Jesus and the Victory of God: Christian Origins and the Question of God* (Minneapolis: Fortress, 1996), 2:273-74.

[5]Gabriel Fackre, *The Christian Story* (Grand Rapids: Eerdmans, 1978), p. 98.

[6]Graham Cole, *God the Peacemaker: How Atonement Brings Shalom* (Downers Grove, IL: InterVarsity Press, 2009), pp. 229-30.

[7]Ibid., p. 230.

[8]Nicholas Wolterstorff, *Until Justice and Peace Embrace* (Grand Rapids: Eerdmans, 1983), p. 72.

[9]I owe this insight and this way of characterizing Jesus' concern to Rikk Watts and his lectures on the Gospel of Mark. See his *The Gospel of Mark: New Testament Book Study*, Regent College, 2000, MP3 audio, available at www.regentaudio.com/products/the-gospel-of-mark-new-testament -book-study.

[10]Neal Plantinga, *Not the Way It's Supposed to Be: A Breviary of Sin* (Grand Rapids: Eerdmans, 1995), p. 199.

[11]Henri Nouwen, *The Wounded Healer: Ministry in Contemporary Society* (New York: Image Books, 1979).

Chapter 5: A Grammar of the Disciplines

[1]Stanley Hauerwas and William Willimon, *Resident Aliens: A Provocative Christian Assessment of Culture and Ministry for People Who Know Something Is Wrong* (Nashville: Abingdon, 1989), p. 97.

[2]Richard Foster, *Life with God: Reading the Bible for Spiritual Transformation* (San Francisco: HarperOne, 2008), p. 17.

[3]Maggie Jackson, *Distracted: The Erosion of Attention and the Coming Dark Age* (Amherst, NY: Prometheus Books, 2009), p. 14.

[4]Leighton Ford, *The Attentive Life: Discerning God's Presence in All Things* (Downers Grove, IL: InterVarsity Press, 2008), p. 23.

[5]Howard Thurman, *The Inward Journey* (Richmond, IN: Friends United Press, 2007), p. 128.

[6]Eugene Peterson, *Subversive Spirituality* (Grand Rapids: Eerdmans, 1997), pp. 6-7.

[7]James Wilhoit, *Spiritual Formation as if the Church Mattered: Growing in Christ Through Community* (Grand Rapids: Baker Academic, 2008), p. 79.

[8]See James M. Kushiner, "Lent: Take Three," *Mere Comments: The Touchstone Blog*, February 22, 2008, touchstonemag.com/merecomments /2007/02/lent_take_three.

[9]James K. A. Smith, *Who's Afraid of Postmodernism: Taking Derrida, Lyotard, and Foucault to Church* (Grand Rapids: Baker Academic, 2006), p. 140.

[10]Karl Heim, *The Nature of Protestantism*, trans. John Schmidt (Minneapolis: Fortress, 1963), p. 79.

[11]Ibid., p. 76.

[12]Adolf von Harnack, quoted in William C. Placher, *Narratives of a Vulnerable God: Christ, Theology and Scripture* (Louisville, KY: Westminster John Knox, 1994), p. 138.

[13]John Calvin, *Institutes of the Christian Religion*, 4.1.4.

[14]Ibid.

[15]Joseph Hellerman, *When the Church Was a Family: Recapturing Jesus' Vision for Authentic Christian Community* (Nashville: B & H Publishing), p. 7.

[16]I'm indebted to my friend and former colleague Markene Meyer for this phrase.

[17]Stanley Hauerwas and William Willimon, *Lord, Teach Us: The Lord's Prayer and the Christian Life* (Nashville: Abingdon, 1996), p. 18.

Chapter 6: Let It Be

[1]Søren Kierkegaard, as quoted by Donald Bloesch, *The Struggle of Prayer* (Colorado Springs: Helmers and Howard, 1988), p. xii.

[2]Richard J. Foster, *The Celebration of Discipline* (San Francisco: HarperSan-Francisco, 1978), p. 33.

[3]William Law, *A Serious Call to a Devout and Holy Life*, Vintage Spiritual Classics (New York: Vintage, 2002), p. 146.

[4]Eugene Peterson, "Prayer," in *Dictionary for the Theological Interpretation of the Bible*, ed. Kevin Vanhoozer (Grand Rapids: Baker Academic, 2005), p. 616.

[5]See Anne Lamott, *Help, Thanks, Wow: The Three Essential Prayers* (New York: Riverhead, 2012).

[6]Simon Chan, *Spiritual Theology: A Systematic Study of the Christian Life* (Downers Grove, IL: IVP Academic, 1998), p. 127.

[7]R. Paul Stevens and Michael Green, *Living the Story: Biblical Spirituality for Everyday Christians* (Grand Rapids: Eerdmans, 2003), p. 110.

[8]Merold Westphal, "Not About Me: Prayer Is the Work of a Lifetime," *Christian Century*, April 5, 2005, p. 20.

[9]Gerald Sittser, *When God Doesn't Answer Your Prayer: Insights to Keep You Praying with Greater Faith and Deeper Hope* (Grand Rapids: Zondervan, 2003), p. 70.

[10]Bloesch, *Struggle of Prayer*, p. 19.

[11]Simone Weil, *Waiting for God*, trans. Emma Craufurd (New York: Harper Colophon, 1951), p. 227.

[12]Karl Barth, *Prayer*, trans. Sara F. Terrien (Louisville, KY: Westminster John Knox, 2002), p. 22.

[13]Ibid., p. 23.

[14]P. T. Forsyth, *The Soul of Prayer* (Vancouver, BC: Regent College Publishing, 2002), p. 30.

[15]Ibid.

[16]Barth, *Prayer*, p. 24.

[17]N. T. Wright, *The Lord and His Prayer* (Grand Rapids: Eerdmans, 1996), p. 15.

[18]Ibid.

[19]Ibid., p. 16.

[20]Stanley Hauerwas and William Willimon, *Lord, Teach Us: The Lord's Prayer and the Christian Life* (Nashville: Abingdon, 1996), p. 34.

[21]Helmut Thielicke, *The Prayer That Spans the World: Sermons on the Lord's*

Prayer, trans. John W. Doberstein (London: James Clarke, 1960), p. 45.

[22]Ibid., p. 48.

[23]Frederick Buechner, *Wishful Thinking: A Seeker's ABC* (New York: Harper-Collins, 1973), p. 60.

[24]Hauerwas and Willimon, *Lord, Teach Us,* p. 66.

[25]Basil the Great, *Speech on Avarice,* available at www.ellopos.net/elpenor/greek-texts/fathers/basil-property.asp?pg=3.

[26]Dietrich Bonhoeffer, *Spiritual Care,* trans. Jay C. Rochelle (Minneapolis: Fortress, 1985), p. 62.

[27]Scot McKnight, *Praying with the Church: Following Jesus Daily, Hourly, Today* (Brewster, MA: Paraclete, 2006), pp. 37-38.

Chapter 7: The Work of the People

[1]Rodney Stark, *The Rise of Christianity* (Princeton, NJ: Princeton University Press, 1996), p. 6.

[2]Minucius Felix, quoted in Alan Kreider, "They Alone Know the Right Way to Live: The Early Church and Evangelism," in *Ancient Faith for the Church's Future,* ed. Mark Husbands and Jeffrey P. Greenman (Downers Grove, IL: InterVarsity Press, 2008), p. 178.

[3]Kreider, "They Alone Know," p. 178.

[4]Debra Rienstra, *So Much More: An Invitation to Christian Spirituality* (San Francisco: Jossey-Bass, 2005), p. 167.

[5]For an excellent and accessible introduction to liturgy for the "liturgically curious," see Mark Galli, *Beyond Smells and Bells: The Wonder and Power of Christian Liturgy* (Brewster, MA: Paraclete, 2008).

[6]William Willimon, *The Service of God: How Worship and Ethics Are Related* (Nashville: Abingdon, 1983), pp. 42-43.

[7]Debra Dean Murphy, *Teaching That Transforms: Worship as the Heart of Christian Education* (Grand Rapids: Brazos, 2004), p. 13.

[8]Michael Frost, *Exiles: Living Missionally in a Post-Christian Culture* (Peabody, MA: Hendrickson, 2006), p. 288.

[9]Alexander Schmemann, *For the Life of the World: Sacraments and Orthodoxy* (Crestwood, NY: St. Vladimir's Seminary Press, 1963), p. 15.

[10]This phrase comes from the South American evangelical theologian C. René Padilla's essay "Spiritual Conflict," in *The New Face of Evangelicalism: An International Symposium on the Lausanne Covenant,* ed. C. René Padilla (Downers Grove, IL: InterVarsity Press, 1976), p. 210.

[11]Murphy, *Teaching That Transforms*, p. 119.

[12]Ibid., p. 127.

[13]Walter Brueggemann, quoted in Murphy, *Teaching That Transforms*, p. 127.

[14]Richard J. Foster, *Celebration of Discipline* (San Francisco: HarperSan-Francisco, 1978), p. 173.

[15]James K. A. Smith, *Desiring the Kingdom: Worship, Worldview and Cultural Formation* (Grand Rapids: Baker Books, 2009), pp. 163-64.

[16]Dietrich Bonhoeffer, *Life Together* and *The Prayer Book of the Bible*, trans. Daniel W. Bloesch and James H. Burtness, Dietrich Bonhoeffer Works (Minneapolis: Fortress, 2005), 5:108.

[17]The Book of Common Worship, quoted in Smith, *Desiring the Kingdom*, p. 179.

[18]Clayton J. Schmidt, *Sent and Gathered: A Worship Manual for the Missional Church* (Grand Rapids: Baker Academic, 2009), p. 170.

[19]Smith, *Desiring the Kingdom*, pp. 181-82.

[20]Jacques Ellul, *The Presence of the Kingdom*, 2nd ed., trans. Olive Wyon (Colorado Springs: Helmers and Howard, 1989), p. 37.

[21]Ibid., pp. 38-39.

[22]Justin Martyr, quoted in Paul Barnett in *Jesus and the Rise of Early Christianity: A History of New Testament Times* (Downers Grove, IL: IVP Academic, 2002), pp. 387-88.

[23]Walter Brueggemann, *Cadences of Home: Preaching Among Exiles* (Louisville, KY: Westminster John Knox, 1997), p. 12.

[24]Ibid.

[25]Søren Kierkegaard, *Kierkegaard's Attack Upon Christendom 1854–1855*, trans. Walter Lowrie (Princeton, NJ: Princeton University Press, 1968), p. 258.

[26]N. T. Wright, *Simply Christian: Why Christianity Makes Sense* (New York: HarperOne, 2006), p. 182.

[27]Frederick Buechner, *Wishful Thinking: A Seeker's ABC* (San Francisco: HarperSanFransisco, 1973), p. 107.

[28]William Willimon, *Worship as Pastoral Care* (Nashville: Abingdon, 1979), p. 168.

[29]Smith, *Desiring the Kingdom*, p. 199.

Chapter 8: Shabbat Shalom

[1]"The Futurist Manifesto," quoted in Carl Honoré, *In Praise of Slowness: How a Worldwide Movement Is Challenging the Cult of Speed* (San Francisco: HarperSanFrancisco, 2004), p. 19.

[2]Honoré, *In Praise of Slowness*, p. 4.

[3]"The Slow Food Manifesto," Slow Food, 2014, www.slowfood.com/about_us/ eng/manifesto.lasso.

[4]Larry Dossey, quoted in Honoré, *In Praise of Slowness*, p. 3.

[5]Timothy Querengesser, "The Slow Lane," *Adbusters*, March 5, 2008.

[6]Dan Allender, *Sabbath*, Ancient Practices Series (Nashville: Thomas Nelson, 2009), p. 7.

[7]Ibid., p. 5.

[8]Lauren Winner, *Mudhouse Sabbath* (Brewster, MA: Paraclete, 2003), p. 11.

[9]Abraham Joshua Heschel, *The Sabbath: Its Meaning for Modern Man* (New York: Farrar, Straus and Giroux, 1951), p. 14.

[10]Ibid.

[11]Ibid., p. 23.

[12]Winner, *Mudhouse Sabbath*, pp. 10-11.

[13]Ruth Haley Barton, *Sacred Rhythms: Arranging Our Lives for Spiritual Transformation* (Downers Grove, IL: InterVarsity Press, 2006), p. 137.

[14]Ibid., p. 138.

[15]Dorothy Bass, "Keeping Sabbath," in *Practicing Our Faith: A Way of Life for a Searching People*, ed. Dorothy Bass (San Francisco: Jossey-Bass, 1997), p. 79.

[16]Heschel, *Sabbath*, pp. 18-19.

[17]Ibid., p. 19.

[18]Allender, *Sabbath*, p. 12.

[19]Heschel, *Sabbath*, p. 18.

[20]Mark Buchanan, *The Rest of God: Restoring Your Soul by Restoring Sabbath* (Nashville: Thomas Nelson, 2006), p. 3.

[21]Allender, *Sabbath*, p. 39.

[22]Ibid., p. 44.

[23]Norman Wirzba, *Living the Sabbath: Discovering the Rhythms of Rest and Delight*, The Christian Practices of Everyday Life Series (Grand Rapids: Brazos, 2006), p. 64.

[24]Augustine, Letter 130: To Proba, 2.4.

[25]Allender, *Sabbath*, p. 61.

[26]Walter Brueggemann, *Cadences of Home: Preaching Among Exiles* (Louisville, KY: Westminster John Knox, 1997), p. 27.

[27]Rodney Clapp, *Border Crossings: Christian Trespasses on Popular Culture and Public Affairs* (Grand Rapids: Brazos, 2000), p. 129.

[28]See Sam Van Eman, *On Earth As It Is in Advertising: Moving from Com-

mercial Hype to Gospel Hope (Grand Rapids: Brazos, 2005).

[29]Susan Maushart, *The Winter of Our Disconnect: How Three Totally Wired Teenagers (and a Mother Who Slept with Her iPhone) Pulled the Plug on Their Technology and Lived to Tell the Tale* (New York: Penguin, 2011), p. 12.

[30]Arthur Paul Boers, *Living into Focus: Choosing What Matters in an Age of Distraction* (Grand Rapids: Brazos, 2012), p. 19.

Chapter 9: Table Manners

[1]Christopher West, *Theology of the Body for Beginners: A Basic Introduction to Pope John Paul II's Sexual Revolution*, rev. ed. (West Chester, PA: Ascension, 2004), p. 11.

[2]See Scot McKnight, *Fasting*, Ancient Practices Series (Nashville: Thomas Nelson, 2009), p. 130. McKnight acknowledges his indebtedness on this point to the outstanding work on this topic done by my former professor and colleague Kent Berghuis. See Kent Berghuis, *Christian Fasting: A Theological Approach* (Dallas: Biblical Studies Press, 2007).

[3]Michael Frost, *The Road to Missional: Journey to the Center of the Church* (Grand Rapids: Baker Books, 2011), p. 36.

[4]Arthur Paul Boers, *Living into Focus: Choosing What Matters in an Age of Distractions* (Grand Rapids: Brazos, 2012), p. 59.

[5]See "Eating Habits of Americans," Graphs.net, www.graphs.net/201208/eating-habits-of-americans.html.

[6]Michael Pollan, *The Omnivore's Dilemma: A Natural History of Four Meals* (New York: Penguin, 2006), p. 11. Later in the book Pollan observes, "Much of our food system depends on our not knowing much about it, beyond the price disclosed by the checkout scanner; cheapness and ignorance are mutually reinforcing. And it's a short way from not knowing who's at the other end of your food chain to not caring—to the carelessness of both producers and consumers that characterizes our economy today. Of course, the global economy couldn't very well function without this wall of ignorance and the indifference it breeds. This is why the American food industry and its international counterparts fight to keep their products from telling even the simplest stories—'dolphin safe,' 'humanely slaughtered,' etc.—about how they were produced. The more knowledge people have about the way their food is produced, the more likely it is that their values—and not just 'value'—will inform their purchasing decisions" (p. 245).

[7]"The Slow Food Manifesto," www.slowfood.com/about_us/eng/manifesto.lasso.

[8]See "About Us," Slow Food USA, 2014, www.slowfoodusa.org/about-us.

[9]Frederick Buechner, *Wishful Thinking: A Seeker's ABC* (San Francisco: Harper SanFrancisco, 1973), p. 25.

[10]John Dominic Crossan, quoted in Craig Blomberg, *Contagious Holiness: Jesus' Meals with Sinners* (Downers Grove, IL: IVP Academic, 2005), p. 97.

[11]Gordon T. Smith, *A Holy Meal: The Lord's Supper and the Life of the Church* (Grand Rapids: Baker Academic, 2005), p. 13.

[12]Christine Pohl, *Making Room: Recovering Hospitality as a Christian Tradition* (Grand Rapids: Eerdmans, 1999), p. 30.

[13]Walter Brueggemann, *Living Toward a Vision: Biblical Reflections on Shalom* (New York: United Church Press, 1976), p. 143. It's unclear in the immediate context whether Brueggemann has the eucharistic table or the dinner table in view. This ambiguity may be intentional. I think it is suggestive.

[14]Dan Allender, *Sabbath*, Ancient Practices Series (Nashville: Thomas Nelson, 2009), p. 14.

[15]McKnight, *Fasting*, p. xx.

[16]Ibid., pp. xxi-xxii.

[17]Augustine, Sermon 210.

[18]John Piper, *A Hunger for God: Desiring God Through Fasting and Prayer* (Wheaton, IL: Crossway, 1997), p. 14.

Chapter 10: Blessed Are the Placemakers

[1]Charles Dickens, *Bleak House* (New York: Signet Classics, 2011), p. 47.

[2]Oliver O'Donovan, "The Loss of a Sense of Place," *The Irish Theological Quarterly* 55, no. 1 (1989): 54.

[3]Eugene Peterson, foreword, in Eric O. Jacobsen, *Sidewalks of the Kingdom: New Urbanism and the Christian Faith* (Grand Rapids: Brazos, 2003), p. 9.

[4]See Kevin J. Vanhoozer, "The World Well Staged? Theology, Culture, and Hermeneutics," in *First Theology: God, Scripture and Hermeneutics* (Downers Grove, IL: InterVarsity Press, 2002), p. 310.

[5]Walter Brueggemann, *Cadences of Home: Preaching Among Exiles* (Louisville, KY: Westminster John Knox, 1997), p. 2.

[6]Bryan Stone, *Evangelism After Christendom: The Theology and Practice of Christian Witness* (Grand Rapids: Brazos, 2007), p. 11.

[7]Ibid.

[8]Brueggemann, *Cadences of Home*, p. 13.

[9]Ibid., pp. 13-14.

[10]See Robert Benson, *A Good Neighbor: Benedict's Guide to Community* (Brewster, MA: Paraclete, 2009).

[11]Albert Hsu, *The Suburban Christian: Finding Spiritual Vitality in the Land of Plenty* (Downers Grove, IL: InterVarsity Press, 2006), p. 60.

[12]Christine Pohl, *Making Room: Recovering Hospitality as a Christian Tradition* (Grand Rapids: Eerdmans, 1999), p. 33.

[13]Ibid.

Conclusion

[1]This reference to Plutarch came to my attention through a series of lectures on leadership by Mark Strom, available at www.regentaudio.com/products/leadership-naming-and-influencing-as-the-image-and-glory-of-God.

[2]Plutarch, quoted in Roy A. Harrisville, *Fracture: The Cross as Irreconcilable in the Language and Thought World of the Biblical Writers* (Grand Rapids: Eerdmans, 2006), p. 87.

Forge

The Forge Missions Training Network exists to help birth and nurture the missional church in America and beyond. Books published by InterVarsity Press that bear the Forge imprint will also serve that purpose.

Beyond Awkward, by Beau Crosetto

Creating a Missional Culture, by JR Woodward

Forge Guides for Missional Conversation (set of five), by Scott Nelson

Incarnate, by Michael Frost

The Missional Quest, by Lance Ford and Brad Brisco

More Than Enchanting, by Jo Saxton

Sentness, by Kim Hammond and Darren Cronshaw

The Story of God, the Story of Us (book and DVD), by Sean Gladding

---

For more information on Forge America, to apply for a Forge residency, or to find or start a Forge hub in your area, visit **www.forgeamerica.com**

For more information about Forge books from InterVarsity Press, including forthcoming releases, visit **www.ivpress.com/forge**